EASY FRUGAL COOKBOOK

EASY FRUGAL
COOKBOOK

100 Satisfying
Recipes That Won't
Break the Bank

Sarah Walker Caron

PHOTOGRAPHY BY ELYSA WEITALA

ROCKRIDGE
PRESS

For general information on our other products and services or to obtain technical support, please contact our Customer Care Department within the United States at (866) 744-2665, or outside the United States at (510) 253-0500.

Rockridge Press publishes its books in a variety of electronic and print formats. Some content that appears in print may not be available in electronic books, and vice versa.

Interior and Cover Designer: Karmen Lizzul
Art Producer: Janice Ackerman
Editor: Myryah Irby
Production Editor: Matt Burnett

Photography: © 2020 Elysa Weitala. Food Styling by Victoria Wollard. P. 133: photograph by Evi Abeler. Author Photo: © 2020 Gabor Degre/Bangor Daily News.

Cover: Salmon Burgers with Avocado, page 91

ISBN: Print 978-1-64611-711-6
eBook 978-1-64611-712-3

R0

For Will and Paige:
May these recipes always remind
you of home.

Also for Zach and Haley:
Food is love.

Contents

Introduction

Shortly after my son was born in 2005, I realized I didn't want to send him to day care just yet. The only alternative I could see to make this a reality was to quit my job. At the time, I was an experienced reporter at a Connecticut daily where I had good sources, good compensation, and a good reputation.

But there was this child who needed me.

I rationalized that even if I quit, I could freelance for the newspaper as many of my mentors had when they'd become parents. It seemed like a no-brainer. Plus, my spouse had a well-paying job that could pick up some of the financial slack.

Fast-forward a few weeks: I'd resigned, lined up freelancing for the paper, and was ready to continue my career. Then everything changed. The well-paying job ended, and I had to take a part-time holiday retail job just to make ends meet. And even then, they didn't really.

After Christmas, my part-time job ended, and I was freelancing in fits and starts. The budget wasn't balancing. New opportunities weren't materializing.

Everything felt like a strain—from buying food for meals to keeping the lights on.

Those were among the hardest months of my adult life.

When it came to groceries, I fed and diapered my son first and relied on coupons, sales, and manager specials on meats that were near expiring. We ate simply. And when something had to give, it was usually my credit card I chose, skipping payments.

About eight months after resigning, just as my son was turning 1, I interviewed for several jobs and was offered one. The influx of income dug me out of the hole I'd landed in—and I swore I would never be there again.

I don't like to think about the budgetary issues of that time. In retrospect, I should have tried to work something out with my job for a graduated return to work instead of simply quitting without a parachute to catch my fall. But we don't get redos. We only get the lessons of our mistakes to ensure we don't make them again.

From that time, I learned some important things about budgeting, stretching the food budget, and making the most of inexpensive, healthy foods to cook from scratch.

Feeding a family is expensive.

When I set out to write this cookbook, I wanted to demystify the process of cooking well while keeping a close eye on costs. In other words, I wanted to write the cookbook I needed as a 26-year-old mother on a shoestring budget. But I also wanted this to be the cookbook I needed to make dinnertime a cinch as a 34-year-old single mom of two, learning to balance life on a single income. And I wanted this to be the cookbook for my 39-year-old self, still raising two kids and now saving for a house. I wanted to write the cookbook for all these selves—all of whom faced financial and time challenges.

> I learned some important things about budgeting, stretching the food budget, and making the most of inexpensive, healthful foods to cook from scratch.

But I also wrote this for budget-strapped people like my brother and sister, who, in college and graduate school, have to make tough choices about what they can afford to eat. And I wrote this for anyone whose shoestring budget has them in need of help stretching their food dollars.

And I wanted to do it while showing that budget-friendly and healthy are not mutually exclusive. You can have both.

I hope, within these pages, you find accessible, succulent, interesting recipes that help you forget, even for a moment, that they are budget-friendly.

|||||||||||||||||||||||||||||||||||||||||||||||||||||||||||||||||||||||||||||||||||||||||||||||||||||||||||||||||||||||||||

CHAPTER ONE

Slashing the Grocery Bill

|||||||||||||||||||||||||||||||||||||||||||||||||||||||||||||||||||||||||||||||||||||||||||||||||||||||||||||||||||||||||||

"What's for dinner?" This familiar refrain echoes in homes throughout the country each night. But, according to the United States Department of Agriculture (USDA), the answer is increasingly takeout or restaurant meals. In 2018, 54.4 percent of money spent on food was spent on food away from home—a 4.3 percent increase from 2009, according to USDA data. Considering that Americans—consumers, businesses, and government entities combined—spent an overall total of $1.71 trillion on food in 2018, according to the USDA, 54.4 percent of that is a lot of money spent on food away from home.

When you want to reduce the overall amount of your food budget, cooking at home is usually the answer. Armed with good, reliable, budget-conscious recipes using whole nutritious foods, you can eat well for less.

Now Serving: Affordable, Delicious Food

Sure, takeout is tempting. Someone else prepares the food and cleans up, and you just sit down to eat it. But nothing beats a delicious meal prepared with love at home—without breaking the bank. Seriously, why order a #5 when you can—in about 30 minutes—have fresh, homemade Hoisin Turkey Lettuce Wraps (page 52) and feed four people for about $10!

Cooking on a Budget

Shopping for groceries on a budget can be tough. There are so many temptations in the grocery store to distract you. But when you get into the habit of eating well, shopping gets easier. And it's important to note that having a food budget doesn't mean eating rice and beans or peanut butter and jelly every night. It also doesn't mean spending all day cooking.

Cooking at home, on a budget, can include dishes like Crispy Coconut Drumsticks (page 89), a favorite of my kids. Served with a veggie, such as steamed broccoli, and a little rice or pasta, it's a complete, balanced meal that can be made for about $5.

Likewise, Country-Fried Steak and Onions (page 108) sounds complicated, but it's made with an inexpensive cut of beef and is a fun, easy meal to serve. Pair with mashed potatoes or pasta, and you have a complete meal for about $10.

Moreover, cooking smartly on a budget can save money. Making a roast chicken? (Might I recommend the Orange-Thyme Roast Chicken [page 78]?) Save the carcass and use it to make Slow Cooker Chicken Stock (page 136). For pennies, you can make your own in a slow cooker (I like to do it overnight) and use it to make Slow Cooker Chicken Tortilla Soup with Lime and Avocado (page 32).

Other suggestions to reduce your food budget include the following:

AVOID PROCESSED AND PREPARED FOODS. A can of soup will feed one—maybe two with a light appetite. But for a few dollars more, you can make a whole pot of soup, feed four, and likely have leftovers for additional meals. In other words, don't be seduced by convenience.

EAT OUT LESS. Commit to eating at home and reserve only one or two meals each month for eating out. Eating at home will help you keep your food budget in check.

PLAN SMARTLY. When planning meals for the week, first take stock of what you have in the pantry, fridge, and freezer. Use these ingredients to select your recipes and shop just for what you need. And don't forget: Leftovers can become part of new meals.

IF YOU DRINK ALCOHOL, REDUCE YOUR ALCOHOL CONSUMPTION. Alcohol can be a budget buster. Instead, limit how much you drink—and choose more cost-effective options when you do. Boxed wine, for instance, has come a long way in recent years.

SET A FOOD BUDGET AND STICK TO IT. When my food spending got out of control recently, I set a food budget to get it in check. At first, it was challenging. But soon, I found myself naturally spending less. It's a little bit monetary Jenga and a little bit creative planning.

Savvy Shopping Strategies

Grocery shopping without a plan is a guarantee to overspend or come home with items you don't really need. Keep these tips in mind to shop smartly.

MAKE A MEAL PLAN. Sit down once a week and plan your meals and the recipes you will use. As you do so, remember to factor in any appointments or events that will change your evenings. For instance, if your child has a concert at school, you may need a superfast dinner that night.

CONSIDER HOW INGREDIENTS CAN BE USED IN MULTIPLE MEALS AND CHOOSE THE CHEAPEST BUT BEST OPTION WHEN PURCHASING. For instance, if you need shredded Cheddar cheese for a recipe, buy a block of cheese. These are often cheaper by the pound than the convenient alternative of something already shredded and can be used for multiple dishes, such as making grilled cheese for lunch or quesadillas for a snack.

MAKE A LIST. You have your recipes and budget. After taking stock of your fridge, freezer, and pantry, make a list of the things you need to make your meals happen. I organize my shopping lists by department so, when shopping, I can check off everything in a section and move to the next one. Don't forget to add foods for breakfasts, lunches, and snacks.

SIGN UP FOR STORE APPS AND LOYALTY CARDS. These often offer coupons for items you typically buy as well as manufacturers' coupons. When loading coupons to your account, make sure any item you select will benefit you—try not to be seduced by discounts on things you don't really need or use.

BE FLEXIBLE AT THE STORE. To make your list fit your budget, you may have to make a series of savvy decisions on the fly. For instance, if you are making a recipe that calls for red bell peppers but yellow bell peppers are on sale, use those instead. If a recipe calls for chicken breasts but tenders are on sale, consider making the swap.

SHOP IN SEASON. In-season produce generally costs less than out-of-season produce. You'll find inexpensive citrus in the winter, strawberries in the spring and summer, and squash in the fall. Also, pay attention to sales on veggies and fruit—stock up and freeze extras to save money in the long run. Depending on what's on sale and what you buy, different processes may be needed for safe freezing. There are numerous online sources for these guidelines, including the USDA.

ONLY WALK THE AISLES THAT CONTAIN ITEMS YOU NEED. This is a good way to limit impulse buying.

KEEP A RUNNING TAB OF EXPENSES. I do this in my head, but you may want to use a calculator to keep yourself on track.

MAKE SMART PROTEIN CHOICES. Again, look for sales and stock up. Choose less expensive cuts when they are available. Sometimes canned chicken or seafood can be substituted in a recipe. And when it comes to seafood, consider buying frozen. Shrimp, in particular, are best bought frozen—the ones in the fish-monger's case are almost always the same as in the freezer compartment, just defrosted for your convenience. And when it comes to beans, dried are almost always less expensive than canned.

GO BIG. Oftentimes you will spend less overall when you buy items in bulk packages. This is particularly true with household paper goods such as paper towels, toilet paper, and tissue, but also true for snacks and even meats—larger bulk packages often are sold at a lesser per-pound rate. When you can, go big and store the items for use later.

DON'T DISCOUNT THE STORE BRAND. Sure, the brand names are what we see in ads and on commercials, but when it comes to frugal shopping, store brands are where it's at. Did you know that store brands are often name-brand items in different packaging? This will save you money overall on your groceries.

HEALTHY, FRUGAL FOOD SWAPS

Convenience in the grocery store comes at a premium—and although it might be a time-saver in the kitchen, it isn't always a benefit for your health. The good news is there are options that offer both convenience and a healthy food choice.

Love an evening snack? Trade your bagged chips for popcorn kernels. Pop them in a paper bag in the microwave (¼ cup kernels for about 2 to 3 minutes on high power). Season with what's on hand: salt, herbs, cheese, butter, or whatever you like.

Skip the pre-cut melon—choose a whole melon. Not only will it be less expensive overall—as in the whole melon costs less than the cup of cut fruit—but you'll also get a lot more fruit to enjoy throughout the week.

Boneless chicken breasts on sale? Skip the luncheon meat. Marinate and cook a few breasts at the beginning of the week to use for lunches. Thinly slice the chicken and use it in sandwiches, salads, soups, and other dishes.

If your grocery store has bulk bins, they can be a great way to get the foods you want at a cheaper price. Oats, nuts, rice, dried beans, and other items can be purchased this way. Even better if they're on sale—and you can stock up or only buy what you need.

Use frozen or fresh veggies interchangeably. Depending on what's in season, fresh or frozen may be less expensive. When fresh veggies are in season, they are inexpensive. But when they are out of season, you pay a premium, so consider frozen instead. Frozen veggies are often flash-frozen so they can be even fresher than out-of-season produce.

The Convenient Kitchen

To get started cooking (or cooking more frequently) at home, prepare your kitchen and stock the key staples and basic cooking equipment you'll need. In the following, you will find my recommendations for necessities as well as some items that are nice to have.

If you are on a tight budget, don't worry. You don't need to buy a lot of new items that you may or may not use. Instead, spend some time cooking and add items as you feel you need them. Also, shop in thrift stores. You can almost always find inexpensive pans and small appliances there for great prices.

Basic Equipment

The following items are key for preparing the recipes in this book. If you don't have them yet, take some time to cook through the recipes using what you have on hand and add to your arsenal of tools as you need or want to.

MUST-HAVE ITEMS

BAKING DISH: Casseroles, desserts, and more can be made in a baking dish. I use a 9-by-13-inch glass baking dish most often, but an 8-by-8-inch glass baking dish is nice to have as a secondary option for smaller batches.

CHEF'S KNIFE: A sharp chef's knife is the workhorse of the kitchen. It can chop, mince, slice, and dice. And having a sharp one is essential—the duller your knife, the more likely you are to be injured by it.

METAL SPATULA: To remove foods from baking sheets and skillets, a metal spatula has the right level of sturdiness and flexibility to get the job done.

RUBBER SPATULA: With this multipurpose tool you can stir, scrape down the sides of bowls, and even use it for pushing things around hot pans. It's particularly good for cooking scrambled eggs.

SAUCEPAN: If you only have one saucepan, a 3-quart size is the most versatile and can handle most jobs in the kitchen. A 1.5-quart saucepan is nice to have, too, but only as a secondary option.

SHEET PAN/BAKING SHEET: From baked chicken breasts to cookies, baking sheets are essential in the kitchen. They come in a variety of sizes. I find the half-sheet size (13-by-18 inches) to be the most useful, but a quarter baking sheet (9-by-13 inches) can work just as well.

SKILLET: For cooking proteins, this is a must. But what kind of skillet? Nonstick or cast iron (which also can be nonstick when cared for properly) is your best bet. A 10-inch skillet is ideal, though a 12-inch and an 8-inch size are nice to have, too.

WHISK: Whisks are great for making vinaigrettes and marinades and for scrambling eggs. A whisk can also be used for sifting flour, making it a quick and simple task.

WOODEN SPOON: When it comes to stirring things on the stove—sauces, soups, and the like—a wooden spoon is my go-to. It's durable and does a good job.

NICE TO HAVE

The following items aren't required for the recipes in this book, but they do make cooking easier.

BLENDER: If you're a fan of smoothies, this is an essential tool, and a high-speed blender is best.

FOOD PROCESSOR: This appliance makes quick work of preparing dips and some sauces as well as chopping ingredients such as nuts and veggies. I have a mini food processor that I use most often.

PARING KNIFE: For smaller jobs like slicing cucumbers or peppers, this is the ideal tool.

SLOW COOKER: This cooking tool can make long-cooking foods, like Slow Cooker Chicken Stock (page 136), and other soups and meals, like Slow Cooker Pulled Turkey Tenderloin with Parsley Pesto (page 82), an easy, hands-off process.

TOASTER OVEN: For toast, melts, and more, a toaster oven saves time and energy—you don't have to heat an entire oven to have a warm meal.

Staple Ingredients

Stocking your fridge and pantry is key to cooking well and avoiding the last-minute urge for takeout when there's "nothing to eat" in the house. The following items are good to keep on hand so you can feel prepared for mealtime. As you peruse this list, consider what you will and will not eat. Don't purchase something you don't like just because it's on this list—substitute what you prefer.

IN YOUR REFRIGERATOR

> Butter, unsalted
> Cheese, such as Cheddar
> Eggs
> Hoisin sauce
> Milk
> Soy sauce

IN YOUR FREEZER

In addition to the food items listed, keep a freezer-safe bag for collecting vegetable scraps from meal prep to make Veggie Scraps Vegetable Stock (page 138).

> Berries, such as raspberries and blueberries
> Chicken
> Ground beef and/or turkey
> Pastas, dried, like tortellini or ravioli
> Shrimp
> Veggies, such as broccoli, corn, peas, and spinach

IN YOUR PANTRY

> Baking powder
> Black pepper, freshly ground
> Bread crumbs
> Canned beans and legumes, such as black beans, cannellini beans, and chickpeas
> Canned tomatoes, such as whole plum tomatoes, diced tomatoes, and tomato paste
> Cinnamon, ground
> Dry mustard
> Flavoring extracts, such as almond and vanilla
> Flour, all-purpose
> Hot sauce
> Lentils, dried
> Nonstick cooking spray
> Oats, old-fashioned
> Oils, such as canola and olive
> Onion powder
> Paprika
> Pasta, dried
> Rosemary, dried
> Salt, kosher
> Sugar, granulated; light brown
> Thyme, dried
> Vinegar, such as apple cider, balsamic, rice, and white wine

MAKE THE MOST OF YOUR TIME

Spending time in the kitchen is an investment—in time and money—so make it worthwhile. Whether you are a new cook or someone who wants to be a more efficient cook, there are ways to economize your time and maximize cooking success. Here are a few easy steps to do just that:

When making a recipe, read the entire recipe—from ingredients to instructions—before you do anything. This allows you to make sure you understand all the steps and are prepared for the workflow of cooking. Also, read any notes or tips on the recipe, as they may offer ideas for substitutions, cooking tips, or other pointers for success.

Gather all your ingredients. This is called "mise en place." By gathering your ingredients before you begin cooking, you prepare yourself for the full task at hand. Moreover, you ensure that you aren't wasting time or energy hunting for ingredients, or running back and forth between cabinets and the refrigerator—or missing any key ingredients needed.

Keep the recipe close at hand. Even though you read the recipe, keep it close by while cooking so you can refer to it as you go. This ensures that you complete all the steps. Also, take note of small tasks like heating pans or turning on the oven. They are often in place in a recipe at a specific time for a reason.

Keeping Food Fresh

Reducing food waste is a fast and easy way to cut your food budget. When you're properly storing and using what you buy, you can be sure your budgetary dollars are being put to their best use. Here's what you need to know to store food properly to reduce food waste:

WHEN STORING MEATS AND OTHER ANIMAL PROTEINS, WRAP THEM PROPERLY. For short-term storage (a few weeks), any airtight packaging, such as a resealable freezer bag or freezer paper, is sufficient for the job. If storing for longer than a few weeks, add an additional protective layer, such as wrapping the food in aluminum foil or plastic wrap, to help prevent freezer burn before putting it in the bag or container.

STORING VEGGIES TO KEEP THEM FRESH VARIES. Onions, potatoes, and winter squash should not be refrigerated but should be kept in a cool, dry place. Leafy greens should be kept in the refrigerator crisper with their ends wrapped in a damp paper towel for maximum life. Brussels sprouts, carrots, celery, cucumbers, leeks, lettuce, peppers, scallions, and summer squash should all be stored in the fridge crisper drawer. Although it's not recommended that large varieties of tomatoes be refrigerated (they can get mealy), they will last longer stored that way, and cherry and grape tomatoes hold up fine when chilled.

LABEL FOOD. Place a piece of masking tape on packages and jot down the date foods were opened or placed in the fridge to help you remember what needs to be used by when.

STORE LEFTOVERS IN AIRTIGHT CONTAINERS. If freezing leftovers, make sure the containers are also freezer-safe. I like to use old marinara jars for this.

WHEN PLANNING TO REHEAT LEFTOVERS FROM DINNER, REFRIGERATE ANY YOU WILL EAT WITHIN A FEW DAYS. Everything else should be frozen in portioned containers.

FOOD	REFRIGERATOR	FREEZER
Bacon	1 week	1 month
Beans, cooked from dried	5 to 7 days	6 months
Chicken	1 to 2 days	9 months
Deli meat	3 to 5 days	1 to 2 months
Eggs, raw (in shell)	3 to 5 weeks	Not recommended
Eggs, hard-boiled (in shell or shelled in airtight container)	1 week	Not recommended
Ground meat	1 to 2 days	1 to 2 months
Hard cheeses, like Cheddar, Parmesan, and Romano	Unopened: 2 to 4 months Opened: 6 weeks	6 months
Soupstew	3 to 4 days	2 to 3 months
Pork	3 to 5 days	4 to 12 months
Sausage, raw	1 to 2 days	1 to 2 months
Sausage, cooked	1 week	1 to 2 months
Steak	3 to 5 days	4 to 12 months
Stock/broth	4 to 5 days	6 to 9 months

Sources: FoodSafety.gov, USDA, TastingTable.com

Sample Meal Plan and Shopping List

This sample meal plan and shopping list is an example of how dinners can be planned to minimize food purchases and food waste while maximizing use of what you buy to stretch each dollar further.

DAY	DINNER
SUN	> Orange-Thyme Roast Chicken (page 78) with a salad and Zesty Orange-Thyme Vinaigrette (page 141); reserve chicken carcass for Slow Cooker Chicken Stock > Make Slow Cooker Chicken Stock (page 136) overnight. > Reserve 1 cup diced Orange-Thyme Roast Chicken for Tuesday's dinner.
MON	> Boneless Pork Chops with Creamy Roasted Red Pepper, Spinach, and Garlic Sauce (page 103) > Use 1 cup Slow Cooker Chicken Stock and freeze the rest. > Store any leftovers in an airtight container.
TUE	> Chicken Tortellini Salad with Roasted Red Pepper Dressing (page 38). > Use 1 cup diced Orange-Thyme Roast Chicken reserved from Sunday. > Store any leftovers in an airtight container.
WED	> Spinach and Tomato Frittata with Feta (page 67) > Store any leftovers in an airtight container.
THU	> Rich Pork Stir-Fry with Hoisin Garlic-Ginger Sauce (page 109) with cooked rice > Store any leftovers in an airtight container.
FRI	> Leftovers night! Lay out your leftovers from the previous nights and serve with a tossed salad.
SAT	> Sheet Pan Garlic Salmon with Roasted Snap Peas (page 80) > Store any leftovers in an airtight container.

Grocery List

In addition to refrigerator and pantry staples (see page 8), you will need the following:

CANNED AND BOTTLED ITEMS

- Roasted red peppers (1 [12-ounce] jar)

DAIRY AND EGGS

- Cheese, feta, crumbled (½ cup)
- Eggs, large (1 dozen)
- Half-and-half (½ cup)
- Yogurt, plain Greek (1 [5.3-ounce] container)

MEAT

- Chicken, roasting (3 to 4 pounds)
- Pork chops, boneless (4 [5-ounce])
- Pork, ground (1 pound)
- Salmon (1 pound)

PANTRY

- Rice of choice (1 [1-pound] bag)

FROZEN FOODS

- Spinach, chopped (2 cups)
- Tortellini, cheese (1 [12-ounce] bag or fresh)

PRODUCE

- Garlic (2 heads)
- Ginger (1-inch piece)
- Lettuce of choice (2 heads)
- Onion (1)
- Orange (1)
- Scallions (1 bunch)
- Shallots (6)
- Sugar snap peas (2 cups)
- Tomatoes, cherry (1 pint)

How to Use This Book

This book provides a blueprint for meals—but don't be afraid to swap a cut of meat for another or to adjust recipes to your tastes. As you work through the recipes, keep an eye on a few things:

> The ⑤ symbol indicates how much the recipe costs to make.

> > ⑤ means about **$5 or less**
> > ⑤ ⑤ means about **$10 or less**
> > ⑤ ⑤ ⑤ means about **$15 or less**

> Each recipe's accompanying Budget Trick can help lower the cost of ingredients.

> Look to the sample meal plan (page 12) and shopping list (page 13) as guides to help you plan your own.

ALSO, CHECK OUT THE RECIPE LABELS:

5 INGREDIENTS: This recipe uses five ingredients or fewer, not counting salt, pepper, and oil.

30 MINUTES: This recipe can be made in 30 minutes or less.

NO-COOK: No cooking required!

ONE POT: This recipe is made using a single pot, pan, skillet, or baking sheet.

AND DIETARY LABELS TO HELP YOU CHOOSE RECIPES ACCORDING TO YOUR NEEDS:

> Dairy-Free

> Gluten-Free

> Nut-Free

> Vegan

> Vegetarian

Broccoli-Scallion
Cheddar Muffins,
PAGE 24

CHAPTER TWO

||||||||||||||||||||||||||||||||||

Breakfast

||||||||||||||||||||||||||||||||||

Turkey, Egg, and Cheese Breakfast Sandwiches

**SERVES 4 | PREP TIME: 5 MINUTES | COOK TIME: 20 MINUTES
(ASSUMING 1 EGG FRIED AT A TIME)**

Growing up in New York, breakfast sandwiches were legion. Built on Kaiser rolls, the warm sandwiches were gooey and satisfying, thanks to the combination of melty cheese, fried egg with a runny yolk, and breakfast meat like bacon or sausage. Pure comfort—and the inspiration for this gooey breakfast sandwich featuring turkey, Cheddar, and that signature fried egg with a runny yolk. Yes, it can be a little messy. But that's the way we like it.

4 ounces thinly sliced deli turkey

½ cup shredded sharp Cheddar cheese

4 hoagie (sub) rolls, split lengthwise

1 tablespoon olive oil, divided

4 large eggs

Salt

Freshly ground black pepper

1. Preheat the oven or a toaster oven to 350°F.

2. Divide the turkey and Cheddar evenly among the rolls and place them on a baking sheet. Toast the sandwiches for 5 to 6 minutes, until the roll is warmed and the cheese is softened.

3. In a skillet over medium heat, heat ¾ teaspoon of olive oil. Add 1 egg (don't break the yolk!) and fry for 4 to 5 minutes, flipping once about halfway through the cooking time, until the white is firm. Top a sandwich with the fried egg and season lightly with salt and pepper. Repeat with the remaining eggs.

BUDGET TRICK: No Cheddar cheese on hand? American cheese makes an excellent substitute on these sandwiches. Use 1 slice per sandwich, tearing it in half so it covers the whole roll.

PER SERVING: Calories: 392; Total fat: 19g; Sodium: 796mg; Carbohydrates: 37g; Fiber: 2g; Sugars: 3g; Protein: 21g.

Roasted Potatoes and Peppers with Scrambled Eggs

SERVES 4 | PREP TIME: 15 MINUTES | COOK TIME: 1 HOUR

Here in Maine, winter breakfasts need to be hearty to fuel us through cold days. And this breakfast—crispy-on-the-outside, soft-on-the-inside potatoes with sweet roasted bell peppers and fluffy scrambled eggs—hits the spot.

1 pound potatoes, such as Yukon Gold, cut into 1-inch chunks

1 bell pepper, any color, cut into 1-inch pieces

1 tablespoon olive oil

Salt

Freshly ground black pepper

2 teaspoons unsalted butter

6 large eggs

¼ cup 2 percent milk

1. Preheat the oven to 400°F. Line a baking sheet with parchment paper.

2. On the prepared baking sheet, toss together the potatoes and bell pepper. Drizzle with the olive oil and season with salt and pepper.

3. Bake for 40 to 50 minutes, stirring every 15 minutes, until the potatoes are cooked through and lightly browned in spots.

4. In a large skillet over medium heat, melt the butter.

5. In a large bowl, whisk the eggs and milk to blend. Season with salt and pepper and whisk again to combine. Pour the eggs into the skillet. Cook for 6 to 8 minutes, stirring, until fluffy and cooked to your desired doneness. Serve the potatoes and peppers topped with the scrambled eggs.

BUDGET TRICK: **Potatoes can last a long time when stored properly, so don't hesitate to buy the cost-effective larger bag and store them in a cool, dry place.**

PER SERVING: Calories: 251; Total fat: 13g; Sodium: 116mg; Carbohydrates: 24g; Fiber: 3g; Sugars: 4g; Protein: 14g.

Peanut Butter–Banana Honey Smoothie

SERVES 4 | PREP TIME: 10 MINUTES

I have two active, athletic kids who are always on the go and often in need of a quick nutrition boost. With protein from the yogurt and peanut butter, potassium from the bananas, and calcium and vitamin D from the milk, this smoothie packs a nutritious punch. Plus, the classic, creamy combination of nutty peanut butter and sweet bananas is always a winner.

1¼ cups vanilla Greek yogurt

4 bananas, peeled

¼ cup peanut butter

2 tablespoons honey

1½ cups 2 percent milk

In a blender, layer the yogurt, bananas, peanut butter, honey, and milk. Blend on high speed, stopping to scrape down the sides of the blender as needed, until smooth. Evenly divide the smoothie among 4 glasses and serve.

BUDGET TRICK: **Don't let overripe bananas go to waste. When bananas are past their prime, peel them, break them in half, and freeze them in a freezer-safe resealable bag. Just grab what you need for recipes like this. Frozen bananas can be used in place of fresh here without defrosting—they will just make a frostier smoothie.**

PER SERVING: Calories: 366; Total fat: 14g; Sodium: 174mg; Carbohydrates: 54g; Fiber: 4g; Sugars: 38g; Protein: 13g.

Raspberry-Almond Smoothie

SERVES 4 | PREP TIME: 10 MINUTES

This might just be my daughter's very favorite smoothie ever because the flavors come at you one at a time. You taste the sweet raspberries first and then the light, fragrant almonds. Finally, the flavor wraps with a pleasant tanginess thanks to the Greek yogurt.

1 cup sliced almonds

2 cups frozen raspberries

1¼ cups vanilla Greek yogurt

1 cup 2 percent milk

2 tablespoons honey

In a blender, combine the almonds, raspberries, yogurt, milk, and honey. Blend on high speed, stopping to scrape down the sides of the blender as needed, until smooth. Evenly divide the smoothie among 4 glasses and serve.

BUDGET TRICK: Buying larger containers of yogurt can be a more cost-effective way to enjoy your favorite probiotic-filled treat. Although the individual containers are convenient, it costs less overall when you buy the large container. In addition to providing portions for recipes like this, you can reuse the containers (or small jars!).

PER SERVING: Calories: 320; Total fat: 16g; Sodium: 80mg; Carbohydrates: 36g; Fiber: 8g; Sugars: 24g; Protein: 13g.

Strawberry-Almond Overnight Oats

SERVES 4 | PREP TIME: 15 MINUTES, PLUS OVERNIGHT SOAKING

Oatmeal lovers who haven't tried overnight oats are missing out. As the oats sit in a mixture of milk, almond extract, and brown sugar, they become creamy, soft, and flavorful. With fresh strawberries and slivers of almond, this easy breakfast is a satisfying combination of sweet, savory, and nutty flavors.

2 cups old-fashioned oats, divided

2 cups 2 percent milk, divided

1 teaspoon almond extract, divided

4 tablespoons light brown sugar, divided

1 cup diced fresh strawberries, divided

½ cup sliced almonds, divided

1. Place 4 half-pint jars on a work surface. In each, combine ½ cup of oats, ½ cup of milk, ¼ teaspoon of almond extract, and 1 tablespoon of brown sugar. Stir well to mix.

2. Top each jar with ¼ cup of strawberries and 2 tablespoons of almonds. Cover the jars and refrigerate overnight. These can be made up to 4 days in advance.

BUDGET TRICK: When strawberries are out of season, frozen strawberries or strawberry jam can be used instead. If using jam, substitute ¼ cup (1 tablespoon of jam per serving). Though I love the texture of diced berries in my oatmeal, the jam provides a nice, smooth swirl of flavor.

PER SERVING: Calories: 333; Total fat: 12g; Sodium: 77mg; Carbohydrates: 51g; Fiber: 6g; Sugars: 19g; Protein: 13g.

Raspberry Oat Muffins

MAKES 12 MUFFINS | PREP TIME: 15 MINUTES | COOK TIME: 20 MINUTES

Muffins are one of my favorite breakfast foods because I can make them ahead and just grab and go—plus, extras freeze well. These muffins are hearty thanks to the oats but still light in texture. And the raspberries create bright, vibrant pockets of sweetness.

1 large egg

1 cup 2 percent milk

½ cup canola oil

2 cups all-purpose flour

½ cup old-fashioned oats, plus 1 tablespoon

½ cup sugar

1 tablespoon baking powder

½ teaspoon salt

1 teaspoon vanilla extract

1½ cups frozen raspberries

1. Preheat the oven to 400°F. Line a standard muffin tin with 12 paper liners.

2. In a large bowl, whisk the egg, milk, and canola oil to blend.

3. Add the flour, ½ cup of oats, the sugar, baking powder, salt, and vanilla. Stir well to combine. Stir in the frozen raspberries. Evenly divide the batter among the prepared muffin cups.

4. Sprinkle the remaining 1 tablespoon of oats over the muffins.

5. Bake for 18 to 20 minutes, until cooked through. A toothpick inserted into the center of a muffin should come out clean.

BUDGET TRICK: **For a taste similar to sometimes pricey vanilla extract, try a dark liquor, like bourbon or dark rum. Or, as long as there are no nut allergies, try almond extract. Raspberry and almond make a delicious match.**

PER SERVING (1 MUFFIN): Calories: 219; Total fat: 10g; Sodium: 237mg; Carbohydrates: 29g; Fiber: 2g; Sugars: 10g; Protein: 4g.

Broccoli-Scallion Cheddar Muffins

MAKES 12 MUFFINS | PREP TIME: 15 MINUTES | COOK TIME: 25 MINUTES

Savory…muffins? Growing up, I never once imagined muffins could be anything but sweet (or at least lightly sweet), but as an adult, I've discovered how good savory takes on sweet baked goods can be. These make a hearty grab-and-go breakfast or easy snack.

1 cup frozen broccoli florets

1 large egg

1 cup 2 percent milk

¼ cup canola oil

2 cups all-purpose flour

1 tablespoon baking powder

1 teaspoon salt

½ teaspoon dry mustard

1 cup shredded Cheddar cheese

2 scallions, sliced

1. Bring a medium pot of water to a boil over high heat. Add the broccoli and cook according to the package directions. Drain.

2. While the broccoli cooks, preheat the oven to 400°F. Line a standard muffin tin with 12 paper liners.

3. In a large bowl, whisk the egg, milk, and canola oil to blend.

4. Add the flour, baking powder, salt, and dry mustard. Stir well to combine.

5. Stir in the Cheddar, cooked broccoli, and scallions to combine. Evenly divide the batter among the prepared cups.

6. Bake for 18 to 22 minutes, or until golden and a toothpick inserted into the center of a muffin comes out clean.

BUDGET TRICK: I love using frozen broccoli florets for these muffins because they are so easy to cook and come in perfectly sized pieces. Cooking them first avoids soggy muffins.

PER SERVING (1 MUFFIN): Calories: 165; Total fat: 8g; Sodium: 396mg; Carbohydrates: 17g; Fiber: 1g; Sugars: 1g; Protein: 6g.

Banana Oat Pancakes

SERVES 4 | PREP TIME: 10 MINUTES | COOK TIME: 25 MINUTES

Pancakes are good. Banana pancakes packed with oats sweetened with brown sugar are even better. These fluffy pancakes are a cinch to make and delightful served with syrup or a dusting of powdered sugar. To keep the pancakes warm while you make them in batches, stick a baking sheet in a 200°F oven and place the pancakes on it as they finish cooking.

1 large egg

1 cup all-purpose flour

1 cup 2 percent milk

½ cup old-fashioned oats

2 tablespoons canola oil

1 tablespoon light brown sugar

1 teaspoon baking powder

Pinch salt

1 banana, mashed

1 teaspoon unsalted butter

1. Place a griddle pan or large skillet over medium heat to warm for 5 minutes so it's good and hot when you are ready to cook the pancakes.

2. In a large bowl, whisk the egg until frothy.

3. Add the flour, milk, oats, canola oil, brown sugar, baking powder, salt, and banana. Beat well to combine.

4. Add the butter to the hot griddle to melt. Drop the batter in ¼-cup rounds onto the hot griddle, leaving ample room between them to maneuver the spatula for flipping.

5. Cook for 6 to 8 minutes, flipping once about halfway through the cooking time, until browned on both sides. Continue until all the batter has been used.

BUDGET TRICK: It's easy to double this recipe and have leftovers. Refrigerate them in an airtight container for 3 to 4 days and heat them in a toaster (like toast!) or in a 325°F toaster oven or regular oven for 4 to 5 minutes until warm.

PER SERVING: Calories: 298; Total fat: 11g; Sodium: 215mg; Carbohydrates: 42g; Fiber: 3g; Sugars: 10g; Protein: 9g.

Ham and Egg Cups with Roasted Red Peppers

SERVES 4 | PREP TIME: 10 MINUTES | COOK TIME: 20 MINUTES

Can a breakfast be both budget-friendly and elegant? Yes—and this special, quick, and easy dish is proof. Slices of deli ham are pressed into muffin cups and filled with cheese and egg. Serve the cups with sweet roasted red peppers for a sunny breakfast treat.

Nonstick cooking spray

8 deli ham slices

½ cup shredded Cheddar cheese

8 large eggs

¼ cup chopped roasted red peppers, divided

Salt

Freshly ground black pepper

1. Preheat the oven to 400°F. Coat 8 cups of a standard muffin tin with nonstick cooking spray.

2. Line each prepared muffin cup by pressing 1 slice of ham into it. Evenly divide the cheese among the cups. Crack 1 egg into each cup.

3. Bake for 14 to 17 minutes until the yolk reaches your desired doneness. (A shorter cooking time produces runnier yolks; cook longer for a firmer yolk.)

4. Let sit for 3 to 4 minutes before loosening the eggs from the cups with a fork and removing them. Top each cup with 1½ teaspoons of roasted red pepper. Season with a light sprinkle of salt and pepper.

BUDGET TRICK: The egg cups as made here do not store well as leftovers. For a make-ahead version scramble the eggs with 2 tablespoons of milk. Evenly divide the eggs among the ham-lined cups with the other ingredients and prepare as directed.

PER SERVING: Calories: 237; Total fat: 15g; Sodium: 472mg; Carbohydrates: 2g; Fiber: <1g; Sugars: 2g; Protein: 21g.

NUT-FREE

Ham, Egg, and Cheese Bake

SERVES 8 | PREP TIME: 10 MINUTES | COOK TIME: 45 MINUTES

Fluffy eggs, savory ham, and sharp Cheddar cheese create a delightful breakfast experience with this egg bake. The secret ingredient, though, is the bread, which almost melts into the eggs. This recipe makes eight servings: four for when you make it and four to save and reheat the next day.

Nonstick cooking spray

8 ounces cubed deli ham

2½ cups cubed leftover French bread (day-old bread is best)

2 cups shredded Cheddar cheese

10 large eggs

1 cup 2 percent milk

1 teaspoon dry mustard

1 teaspoon garlic powder

½ teaspoon salt

1. Preheat the oven to 350°F. Coat a 9-by-13-inch glass baking dish with nonstick cooking spray.

2. Spread the ham and bread cubes in the prepared dish. Top with the cheese, distributing it evenly.

3. In a large bowl, whisk the eggs, milk, dry mustard, garlic powder, and salt to blend. Pour the mixture over the ham, bread, and cheese, taking care to pour it all over, coating the bread.

4. Bake for 40 to 45 minutes until golden brown. Remove from the oven and let cool for a few minutes before cutting into 8 pieces. Refrigerate leftovers in an airtight container for 1 to 2 days.

BUDGET TRICK: **If you don't have leftover French bread, any leftover bread will do. Try to use a variety that isn't sweet, though, such as rye, sourdough, ciabatta, or Italian. Sweeter breads (like many white breads or raisin bread) will alter the flavor of the finished dish.**

PER SERVING: Calories: 282; Total fat: 17g; Sodium: 726mg; Carbohydrates: 8g; Fiber: <1g; Sugars: 4g; Protein: 22g.

Slow Cooker Chicken
Tortilla Soup with
Lime and Avocado,
PAGE 32

CHAPTER THREE

Soups and Salads

Spicy Chipotle Butternut Squash Soup

SERVES 4 | PREP TIME: 15 MINUTES | COOK TIME: 1 HOUR

They say perfection takes time, and that is true in the case of this bold soup with big flavors. Sweet butternut squash blends with warm cinnamon and spicy chipotle peppers for a delightful, creamy bowl that will please all the spice lovers in the family. This soup is excellent served with something crispy on the side.

2 tablespoons olive oil

1 sweet onion, diced

2 carrots, diced

1 butternut squash, peeled, halved, seeded, and cubed

2 canned chipotle peppers in adobo sauce

1 tablespoon adobo sauce (from the can), plus more as needed

4 cups Veggie Scraps Vegetable Stock (page 138) or store-bought vegetable broth

1 teaspoon ground cinnamon, plus more as needed

Salt

Freshly ground black pepper

1. In a large pot or Dutch oven over medium heat, heat the olive oil. Add the onion and cook for 10 to 12 minutes, until softened and beginning to brown.

2. Stir in the carrots, squash, chipotle peppers, and adobo sauce. Cook for 3 minutes.

3. Add the vegetable stock, cover the pot, and cook for 30 minutes, or until the vegetables are fork-tender.

4. Stir in the cinnamon. Taste and season with salt and pepper. Re-cover the pot and simmer for 10 minutes more. Remove from the heat. Using a stick blender, puree the soup in the pot until smooth. Alternatively, carefully transfer the soup to a standard blender, working in batches as needed, and puree until smooth. Be very careful when blending hot soup, ensuring that the blender is only partially filled and the top is on, as the hot soup can scald.

BUDGET TRICK: This soup freezes beautifully—it will keep frozen for 4 to 6 weeks.

PER SERVING: Calories: 170; Total fat: 8g; Sodium: 143mg; Carbohydrates: 26g; Fiber: 8g; Sugars: 7g; Protein: 3g.

DAIRY-FREE | GLUTEN-FREE | NUT-FREE | ONE POT | VEGAN

Easy Spinach-Lentil Soup

SERVES 4 | PREP TIME: 15 MINUTES | COOK TIME: 35 MINUTES

Lentils are inexpensive, cook quickly from dried, and provide a meat-like quality to dishes. Plus, they work well with many flavors. In this soup, brown lentils, which hold their shape when cooked, join onion, garlic, spinach, and seasonings to make a light, earthy soup perfect for chilly days. Note: If you use store-bought broth, this recipe will cost slightly more.

1 tablespoon olive oil

1 large yellow onion, diced

3 garlic cloves, minced

2 teaspoons paprika

2 teaspoons dried rosemary

4 cups Veggie Scraps Vegetable Stock (page 138) or store-bought vegetable broth

2 cups water

2 cups frozen cut leaf spinach

1½ cups dried brown lentils, rinsed and picked over

Salt

Freshly ground black pepper

1. In a large pot or Dutch oven over medium heat, heat the olive oil. Add the onion and cook for 10 to 12 minutes, until it begins to brown. Add the garlic and cook for 1 minute.

2. Add the paprika, rosemary, vegetable stock, water, spinach, and lentils. Cover the pot and cook for 20 minutes, or until the lentils are tender. Taste and season with salt and pepper.

BUDGET TRICK: **Although lentils keep well in the pantry, buying from the bulk bins is always smart. Not only will it cost less than individual bags of dried lentils, but the lentils will often be fresher, too. And you can purchase only as much as you need!**

PER SERVING: Calories: 332; Total fat: 9g; Sodium: 79mg; Carbohydrates: 46g; Fiber: 23g; Sugars: 5g; Protein: 21g.

Slow Cooker Chicken Tortilla Soup with Lime and Avocado

SERVES 4 | PREP TIME: 15 MINUTES | COOK TIME: 10 HOURS

This delightful soup is tangy, filling, and packed with flavors I love. The creamy avocado, meaty black beans, tomatoes, and chicken taste perfect together. And the hearty dose of cilantro is the ideal fresh garnish. Most of all, though, I love how easy it is to dump the ingredients into the slow cooker and come home to a piping-hot soup almost ready to serve.

1 yellow onion, diced

3 garlic cloves, minced

4 cups Slow Cooker Chicken Stock (page 136) or store-bought chicken broth

1 (14.5-ounce) can diced tomatoes

1 (10-ounce) can diced tomatoes with green chilies

1 (14.5-ounce) can black beans, rinsed and drained

1. In a slow cooker, combine the onion, garlic, chicken stock, diced tomatoes, tomatoes with green chilies, black beans, and chicken. Cover the cooker and cook on low heat for 8 to 10 hours, until the chicken is cooked through.

2. Using two forks, shred the chicken.

3. Juice 1½ of the limes and add the juice to the slow cooker, reserving the remaining lime half. Stir in the cilantro, avocado, and tortilla strips.

4. Cut the remaining lime half into 4 wedges. Serve the soup with a lime wedge for squeezing.

BUDGET TRICK: **If chicken breasts are outside your budget, use boneless chicken thighs. Just trim any visible fat before cooking or the soup will be greasy. Prepare as directed.**

1 pound boneless, skinless chicken breast, trimmed

2 limes, divided

1 cup roughly chopped fresh cilantro

1 avocado, peeled, halved, pitted, and diced

2 (6-inch) corn tortillas, cut into strips

COOKING TIP: This recipe is intended for the slow cooker, which is the preferred method of cooking. However, to prepare it on the stovetop, in a large pot or Dutch oven over medium heat, heat 1 tablespoon of olive oil. Add the onion and garlic and cook, stirring occasionally, for 10 to 12 minutes, or until the onion begins to brown. Add the chicken stock, diced tomatoes, tomatoes with green chilies, black beans, and chicken to the pot and bring to a boil. Reduce the heat to medium-low, cover the pot, and cook for about 45 minutes, or until the chicken can be easily shredded with two forks. Finish the recipe as instructed in steps 3 and 4.

PER SERVING: Calories: 427; Total fat: 13g; Sodium: 556mg; Carbohydrates: 41g; Fiber: 14g; Sugars: 6g; Protein: 39g.

DAIRY-FREE | GLUTEN-FREE | NUT-FREE | ONE POT

Sweet and Sour Cabbage Kielbasa Soup

SERVES 4 | PREP TIME: 15 MINUTES | COOK TIME: 55 MINUTES

Of all the soups in this book, my kids look forward to this one the most—and they can't get enough. With its rich broth, this soup is filled with onion, cabbage, and tomato, and finished with slices of flavorful kielbasa. The seasonings in the broth—garlic, brown sugar, and apple cider vinegar—transform the soup into a sweet-sour-savory delight. Serve with slices of crusty bread for sopping up the flavorful broth.

1 tablespoon olive oil

2 carrots, diced

1 sweet onion, diced

3 garlic cloves, minced

1 small head cabbage, quartered and thinly sliced

4 cups Slow Cooker Chicken Stock (page 136) or store-bought chicken broth

1 (14.5-ounce) can diced tomatoes with their juices

2 tablespoons light brown sugar

2 tablespoons apple cider vinegar

1 (about 13-ounce) kielbasa, sliced

1. In a large pot or Dutch oven over medium heat, heat the olive oil. Add the carrots and onion. Cook for 10 to 12 minutes, stirring occasionally, until softened. Stir in the garlic and cook for 1 minute until fragrant.

2. Stir in the cabbage, chicken stock, tomatoes, and brown sugar. Cover the pot and cook for 30 minutes.

3. Stir in the vinegar and kielbasa. Re-cover the pot and cook for 10 minutes more to heat the kielbasa.

BUDGET TRICK: **Look for kielbasa on sale at the grocery store to stock up. It freezes exceptionally well and will keep, frozen, for 1 to 2 months.**

PER SERVING: Calories: 477; Total fat: 31g; Sodium: 1,222mg; Carbohydrates: 30g; Fiber: 6g; Sugars: 19g; Protein: 22g.

Vegetable Beef Soup

SERVES 4 | PREP TIME: 20 MINUTES | COOK TIME: 1 HOUR 30 MINUTES

The longer cooking time for this soup does something magical to the ingredients, transforming the individual flavors into a rich, decadent soup with so-tender beef. A rich bowl of homemade soup is lovely and filling for lunch or dinner served with crusty bread or rolls.

1 tablespoon olive oil

1 large sweet onion, diced

1 pound stew beef, cut into 1-inch or smaller pieces

2 celery stalks, cut into ¼-inch pieces

2 carrots, diced

3 potatoes, scrubbed and diced

4 cups beef stock

1 (28-ounce) can plum tomatoes, tomatoes chopped and juices reserved

Salt

Freshly ground black pepper

1. In a large pot or Dutch oven over medium heat, heat the olive oil. Add the onion and cook for 8 to 10 minutes, stirring occasionally, until softened and beginning to brown.

2. Stir in the stew beef. Increase the heat to medium-high and cook for 4 to 5 minutes, stirring occasionally, until browned on all sides. The beef will not be cooked through.

3. Add the celery, carrots, potatoes, beef stock, tomatoes with their juices, 1 teaspoon of salt, and ¼ teaspoon of pepper. Reduce the heat to medium and cover the pot. Cook for 30 minutes, stirring occasionally. Reduce the heat to medium-low and cook for 30 to 40 minutes more, until the vegetables are very tender and the meat is fall-apart tender. Taste and season with more salt and pepper as needed.

BUDGET TRICK: This recipe calls for stew beef, which is often the cheapest cut of beef. However, if a better cut, like sirloin, is available for less, then buy it and cut it into chunks.

PER SERVING: Calories: 418; Total fat: 10g; Sodium: 1,215mg; Carbohydrates: 43g; Fiber: 9g; Sugars: 14g; Protein: 37g.

Lemony Vegetable Quinoa Soup

SERVES 4 | PREP TIME: 15 MINUTES | COOK TIME: 45 MINUTES

Robust with vegetables, this filling soup has a tangy flavor thanks to the tomatoes and lemon juice. It's a lovely, refreshing, bone-warming dish that pairs well with crusty bread for sopping up the broth.

1 tablespoon olive oil

1 onion, diced

1 red bell pepper, diced

1 green bell pepper, diced

2 celery stalks, thinly sliced

4 garlic cloves, minced

1 (28-ounce) can plum tomatoes, tomatoes chopped and juices reserved

4 cups Veggie Scraps Vegetable Stock (page 138) or store-bought vegetable broth

½ cup dried quinoa, rinsed

1 teaspoon dried thyme

1 teaspoon dried rosemary

Salt

Freshly ground black pepper

Juice of 1 lemon

1. In a large pot or Dutch oven over medium heat, heat the olive oil. Add the onion, red and green bell peppers, and celery. Cook for 8 to 10 minutes, stirring occasionally, until softened. Stir in the garlic and cook for about 1 minute until fragrant.

2. Add the tomatoes and their juices, vegetable stock, quinoa, thyme, and rosemary. Stir well. Cover the pot and cook for 25 to 30 minutes, until the quinoa is cooked through and the vegetables are uniformly tender. Taste and season with salt and pepper as needed.

3. Stir in the lemon juice and serve.

BUDGET TRICK: Reserve vegetable scraps from this recipe in a bag in the freezer so you can make another batch of Veggie Scraps Vegetable Stock (page 138) to replenish the batch you use here.

PER SERVING: Calories: 222; Total fat: 5g; Sodium: 420mg; Carbohydrates: 37g; Fiber: 8g; Sugars: 13g; Protein: 7g.

Warm Brussels Sprouts Salad with Pear and Red Onion

SERVES 4 | PREP TIME: 15 MINUTES | COOK TIME: 15 MINUTES

Tender Brussels sprouts, sweet pear chunks, tart pomegranate arils—this warm salad combines a variety of flavors and textures, married with the tart lemony vinaigrette. It's delicious on its own but also excellent served with chicken or herbed white beans.

3 tablespoons olive oil, divided

1 pound Brussels sprouts, ends trimmed, cut into coins

¼ cup thinly sliced red onion, slices quartered

1 garlic clove, minced

1 pear, diced

¼ cup pomegranate arils

Grated zest of 1 lemon

Juice of 1 lemon

¼ teaspoon dry mustard

Salt

Freshly ground black pepper

1. In a skillet over medium heat, heat 1 tablespoon of olive oil. Add the Brussels sprouts, red onion, and garlic. Cook for 10 to 12 minutes, stirring occasionally, until tender and browned. Transfer the Brussels sprouts mixture to a large bowl. Add the pear and pomegranate arils and toss to combine.

2. In a small bowl, whisk the lemon zest, lemon juice, remaining 2 tablespoons of olive oil, and dry mustard to blend. Drizzle the dressing over the Brussels sprouts and toss to coat. Taste and season with salt and pepper as needed.

BUDGET TRICK: This is best made when Brussels sprouts are in season (late fall and most of winter), when they are the most flavorful and least expensive.

PER SERVING: Calories: 176; Total fat: 11g; Sodium: 29mg; Carbohydrates: 20g; Fiber: 6g; Sugars: 9g; Protein: 4g.

Chicken Tortellini Salad with Roasted Red Pepper Dressing

SERVES 4 | PREP TIME: 10 MINUTES | COOK TIME: 10 MINUTES

Sweet roasted red peppers combine with zesty garlic and a touch of oil and vinegar to make a robust, piquant dressing for this pasta salad. Use any cooked chicken you have (canned works, too!) with your favorite cheese tortellini for a hearty and satisfying dish. Serve warm or chilled, though I do prefer it warm.

1 (12-ounce) package cheese tortellini, fresh or frozen

1 cup diced chicken (leftover, rotisserie, or canned)

2 scallions, thinly sliced

⅓ cup roasted red peppers

1 garlic clove, chopped

1 tablespoon olive oil

1 tablespoon white wine vinegar

Salt

Freshly ground black pepper

1. Cook the tortellini according to the package directions. Drain and transfer to a large bowl. Gently stir in the chicken and scallions. Mix well.

2. In a blender, combine the roasted red peppers, garlic, olive oil, and vinegar. Blend until smooth. Drizzle the dressing over the tortellini mixture and toss well to combine. Taste and season with salt and pepper as needed.

BUDGET TRICK: Frozen cheese tortellini are tasty and affordable. Stock up when you find a sale. They can be used in many ways, including as an easy side dish paired with chicken, in a variety of salads, in soups like Vegetable Beef Soup (page 35), and as the base of a quick dinner topped with Easy Marinara Sauce (page 145).

PER SERVING: Calories: 272; Total fat: 14g; Sodium: 488mg; Carbohydrates: 19g; Fiber: 2g; Sugars: 3g; Protein: 17g.

5 INGREDIENTS | 30 MINUTES | DAIRY-FREE | GLUTEN-FREE | NUT-FREE | ONE POT | VEGAN

Warm Balsamic Red Cabbage Salad

SERVES 4 | PREP TIME: 10 MINUTES | COOK TIME: 20 MINUTES

With just four ingredients (not counting salt), this salad sounds simple. Sautéing the cabbage and finishing with balsamic vinegar transforms it into something robustly wonderful. I love to eat this salad alone, but it's also delightful with sautéed fish or poultry.

1 tablespoon olive oil

4 cups shredded red cabbage

1½ cups diced red onion

Salt

2 to 3 tablespoons balsamic vinegar

1. In a large skillet over medium heat, heat the olive oil. Add the red cabbage and red onion to the skillet. Cook for 10 to 12 minutes, stirring occasionally, until softened.

2. Season with 1 teaspoon of salt and stir well.

3. Drizzle the salad with balsamic vinegar and cook for 3 to 5 minutes more, stirring occasionally, until the liquid evaporates.

BUDGET TRICK: Leftover red onion can be refrigerated in an airtight container for 5 to 6 days. Sliced thinly, red onion adds a crunch and flavor punch to sandwiches and salads. It can also be used in recipes such as stir-fries or baked into a frittata or quiche.

PER SERVING: Calories: 79; Total fat: 4g; Sodium: 23mg; Carbohydrates: 11g; Fiber: 3g; Sugars: 5g; Protein: 2g.

Deli Meat Salad

SERVES 4 | PREP TIME: 15 MINUTES

When a sandwich-only deli in my city transformed its New Jersey–themed subs into salads, a coworker excitedly showed me her "meat salad." And I was all in. It had transformed the sandwiches I'd come to love into a lighter but still filling alternative. This salad is flexible—use whatever deli meat and cheese you like (Ham and Swiss! Turkey and provolone! Roast beef and Cheddar!) and your favorite vinaigrette to turn a favorite sandwich into a new favorite salad.

8 cups chopped lettuce of choice

1 cup chopped fresh tomato

¼ cup sliced banana peppers, drained

4 slices deli cheese of choice

8 ounces thin-sliced deli meat of choice

Thinly sliced red onion, for garnish (optional)

Sliced black olives, for garnish (optional)

Shredded carrot, for garnish (optional)

Zesty Orange-Thyme Vinaigrette (page 141) or bottled dressing of choice, for serving

1. Evenly divide the lettuce among 4 plates or bowls. Top each with an equal amount of tomato, banana peppers, and any other veggies you wish to use.

2. Working with 1 slice of cheese at a time, roll it into a cylinder and thinly slice it crosswise. Place the slices from 1 piece of cheese on each salad.

3. Evenly divide the deli meat into 4 portions and roll each portion into a cylinder. Thinly slice each portion crosswise and add to each salad.

4. Garnish with any optional ingredients, and dress with the vinaigrette for serving.

BUDGET TRICK: To keep the cost down, shop deli sales. Prices can be reduced by half (or more!) when deli meats and cheeses are on sale.

PER SERVING, USING ROMAINE, SWISS & TURKEY WITHOUT DRESSING: Calories: 157; Total fat: 6g; Sodium: 620mg; Carbohydrates: 8g; Fiber: 3g; Sugars: 2g; Protein: 16g.

Roasted Vegetable Orzo Salad with Red Wine Vinaigrette

SERVES 4 | PREP TIME: 15 MINUTES | COOK TIME: 35 MINUTES

"I love orzo!" my daughter proclaimed at least a dozen times between when I bought the diminutive pasta and when I made this dish. Tender roasted veggies, a tart red wine vinaigrette, and orzo combine to make a satisfying, easy salad, enjoyed hot or cold.

FOR THE RED WINE VINAIGRETTE

3 tablespoons red wine vinegar

2 tablespoons olive oil

¼ teaspoon dry mustard

Salt

Freshly ground black pepper

FOR THE SALAD

1 bunch scallions, cut into ½-inch pieces

3 cups broccoli florets

1 red bell pepper, cut into ½-inch squares

1 tablespoon olive oil

Salt

Freshly ground black pepper

8 ounces dried orzo

1. Preheat the oven to 425°F.

TO MAKE THE RED WINE VINAIGRETTE

2. In a small bowl, whisk the vinegar, olive oil, and dry mustard until well combined. Taste and season with salt and pepper and whisk again to blend. Set aside.

TO MAKE THE SALAD

3. Arrange the scallions, broccoli, and red bell pepper on a baking sheet. Drizzle with olive oil and season with salt and pepper.

4. Bake for 20 minutes. Stir well. Bake for 10 to 15 minutes more, until the vegetables are tender.

5. Meanwhile, cook the orzo according to the package directions. Drain.

6. In a large bowl, combine the roasted vegetables and orzo. Drizzle with the vinaigrette and toss to combine. Taste and season with more salt and pepper as needed.

CONTINUED

BUDGET TRICK: Did you know that grocery store brands are often name brands packaged in generic packaging? At the grocery store I frequent, the store-brand pasta seems to be from one of the best pasta brands—and costs 30 to 40 percent less than the name brand (depending on time of year).

PER SERVING: Calories: 328; Total fat: 12g; Sodium: 19mg; Carbohydrates: 49g; Fiber: 5g; Sugars: 4g; Protein: 8g.

Garlic-Ginger Cauliflower Salad

SERVES 4 | PREP TIME: 10 MINUTES | COOK TIME: 45 MINUTES

The vibrant flavors of garlic and ginger transform creamy cauliflower into a scrumptious topping for a bed of lettuce—no dressing needed! My daughter was a little skeptical when I told her that this salad was dressing-less, but after trying it for lunch one day, she was pleasantly surprised—and ate all the leftovers. The cauliflower can be enjoyed hot or cold. To make it gluten-free, use tamari in place of soy sauce.

1 head cauliflower, broken into florets

½ cup diced red onion

1 tablespoon grated peeled fresh ginger

3 garlic cloves, minced

2 tablespoons olive oil

1 teaspoon salt

1 tablespoon soy sauce

4 cups torn lettuce of choice, such as mesclun greens, romaine, iceberg, or butter

1. Preheat the oven to 425°F. Line a baking sheet with parchment paper. Set aside.

2. In a large bowl, stir together the cauliflower, red onion, ginger, garlic, and olive oil. Spread the mixture on the prepared baking sheet and season it with the salt.

3. Bake for 25 minutes. Stir well. Bake for 10 to 12 minutes more until the vegetables are browned and softened.

4. Drizzle the vegetable mixture with the soy sauce. Stir well to coat. Bake for 5 minutes more until the florets are tender and browned.

5. Arrange the lettuce on 4 plates. Top each with one-fourth of the cauliflower mixture. (The cauliflower can also be made in advance and enjoyed cold on the lettuce.)

BUDGET TRICK: Fresh ginger is a flavor enhancer for dishes like this. But it's also perishable. When you buy it, peel it completely and place it in a freezer-safe container. It can be grated from frozen for use, and freezing extends its useful life.

PER SERVING: Calories: 118; Total fat: 8g; Sodium: 856mg; Carbohydrates: 12g; Fiber: 5g; Sugars: 4g; Protein: 4g.

Open-Face Turkey Cranberry
Sandwiches with
Pepper Jack Cheese,
PAGE 48

Sandwiches and Wraps

Chicken Caprese Wraps

SERVES 4 | PREP TIME: 10 MINUTES

Caprese—that lovely combination of bright basil, creamy mozzarella, and juicy tomato—is a favorite that reminds me of summer days and alfresco dining. In this wrap version, those flavors are combined with sweet roasted red peppers, meaty chicken, and crisp lettuce. It's a tasty ode to summertime that packs well for lunches.

4 large sandwich wraps

⅓ cup Basil-Walnut Pesto (page 143) or store-bought pesto

8 ounces fresh mozzarella cheese, sliced

1 tomato, sliced

½ cup sliced roasted red peppers

1 cup sliced, diced, or shredded cooked chicken

1 cup shredded lettuce

1. Place the wraps on a work surface or cutting board. Evenly divide the pesto among them, spreading it in a line down the center of the wraps. Top each wrap with an equal amount of mozzarella, tomato, roasted red peppers, chicken, and lettuce.

2. Roll in the ends of the wrap, and then turn and roll it into a cylinder, taking care to tuck in the ends as you go. Secure with toothpicks and halve each wrap for serving.

BUDGET TRICK: Whether you buy or make pesto, don't let leftovers go to waste. Toss it with pasta, spread it on burgers, top crackers with it, and more. Or freeze leftovers for another day. Leftover pesto should be eaten within 1 week.

PER SERVING: Calories: 485; Total fat: 25g; Sodium: 617mg; Carbohydrates: 34g; Fiber: 6g; Sugars: 3g; Protein: 28g.

Italian Sausage Sandwiches with Apple and Red Cabbage Slaw ⓢ ⓢ

SERVES 4 | PREP TIME: 10 MINUTES | COOK TIME: 20 MINUTES

When I was little, my grandmother would make big trays of sausage and peppers for family dinners, and while she was making them, I would steal pieces of sausage—with her sort-of blessing. In this dish, juicy, hot sausages are topped with a sweet-tart slaw and served on a roll. They're fulfilling and modern. Plus, they're easy!

1 pound
   Italian sausage

½ cup water

2 cups finely shredded
   red cabbage

1 Granny Smith apple,
   cut into matchsticks

¼ cup thinly sliced
   red onion, slices
   quartered

3 tablespoons apple
   cider vinegar

2 tablespoons
   canola oil

1 teaspoon sugar

Salt

Freshly ground
   black pepper

4 hoagie rolls, slit
   lengthwise

1. In a large skillet over medium heat, combine the sausage with the water. Cover the skillet and bring to a boil. Cook for 10 minutes. Remove the cover and cook, turning, for 5 to 7 minutes more, until thoroughly browned on all sides.

2. Meanwhile, make the slaw. In a large bowl, combine the red cabbage, apple, and red onion. Stir well.

3. In a small bowl, whisk the vinegar, canola oil, and sugar to blend. Taste and season with salt and pepper. Pour the dressing over the red cabbage mixture. Toss well to coat. Let sit for at least 10 minutes before using. (This can be made in advance and refrigerated in an airtight container until needed—the flavors improve the longer it sits.)

4. Divide the sausages evenly among the rolls and top with the tangy slaw.

BUDGET TRICK: **You'll likely have extra slaw. Refrigerate it in an airtight container for 3 to 4 days.**

PER SERVING: Calories: 602; Total fat: 36g; Sodium: 1,365mg; Carbohydrates: 46g; Fiber: 4g; Sugars: 11g; Protein: 24g.

Open-Face Turkey Cranberry Sandwiches with Pepper Jack Cheese

SERVES 4 | PREP TIME: 5 MINUTES | COOK TIME: 10 MINUTES

Open-face sandwiches are great for stretching the end of a loaf of bread, and they somehow feel fancier than their two-slice counterparts. The other benefit to open-face sandwiches is you can add a very wet ingredient, like cranberry sauce. This particular dish is something my family loves to make when we are time-crunched and hungry.

4 slices rye bread

8 ounces sliced roasted deli turkey

4 slices pepper Jack cheese

⅓ cup whole berry cranberry sauce

1. Toast the bread.

2. Preheat the oven to 350°F.

3. Arrange the toast slices on a baking sheet. Evenly divide the turkey among them, draping the slices on top. Top each with 1 slice of pepper Jack cheese.

4. Bake for 8 to 10 minutes, until the cheese is melted. Transfer each sandwich to a separate plate and top each with one-fourth of the cranberry sauce.

BUDGET TRICK: Leftover cranberry sauce is great for enjoying on toast or other sandwiches. It can also be eaten with pork chops for a tasty alternative to applesauce. Looking for something different? Add a cranberry layer to quick breads or muffins. Or for a sweet-tart-spicy salsa, stir in 1 minced jalapeño, ¼ cup chopped red onion, and 2 tablespoons of freshly squeezed lime juice to 1 cup of leftover cranberry sauce.

PER SERVING: Calories: 239; Total fat: 7g; Sodium: 955mg; Carbohydrates: 28g; Fiber: 2g; Sugars: 9g; Protein: 16g.

DAIRY-FREE | NUT-FREE | ONE POT

Sheet Pan Teriyaki Beef Subs with Red Peppers and Pineapple

SERVES 4 | PREP TIME: 15 MINUTES, PLUS 30 MINUTES TO MARINATE |
COOK TIME: 20 MINUTES

A simple combination of ingredients can create something unexpectedly delight-ful. That's the case with this sandwich—flavorful marinated meat, sweet pineapple, and tender red bell peppers. I love it all piled together on rolls! The longer you marinate the London broil, the better. The teriyaki sauce tenderizes and flavors the inexpensive cut of meat for a result that eats more like an expensive cut.

1 pound London broil steak

½ cup teriyaki sauce

1 red bell pepper, thinly sliced

1 cup pineapple chunks

Nonstick cooking spray

Salt

4 hoagie rolls, slit lengthwise

1 cup shredded lettuce

1. In a large container or resealable bag, combine the London broil and teriyaki sauce. Cover and chill for at least 30 minutes, turning once. A longer mar-inating time results in a deeper flavor—feel free to marinate for hours, if you have the time.

2. Preheat the broiler. If your broiler has high and low settings, preheat it to high. Line a baking sheet with aluminum foil.

3. Remove the London broil from the marinade and place the steak on the prepared baking sheet.

4. Broil for 9 minutes. Remove the pan from the oven and flip the London broil. Arrange the red bell pepper and pineapple around it. Spritz the bell pepper and pineapple with nonstick cooking spray and season with a pinch of salt. Broil for 9 to 12 minutes more or to your desired doneness.

CONTINUED

5. Transfer the London broil to a cutting board and let sit for 10 minutes before cutting it thinly against the grain into slices.

6. Divide the London broil evenly among the rolls, topping each with one-fourth of the red bell pepper and pineapple chunks. Finish each sandwich with ¼ cup of shredded lettuce.

BUDGET TRICK: The rolls can be the most expensive part of this meal. For a less expensive but no less delicious option, serve this over lettuce or rice.

PER SERVING: Calories: 439; Total fat: 13g; Sodium: 1,637mg; Carbohydrates: 46g; Fiber: 3g; Sugars: 12g; Protein: 35g.

Grilled Ham, Cheese, and Tomato Sandwiches

SERVES 4 | PREP TIME: 5 MINUTES | COOK TIME: 20 MINUTES

For this sandwich, my kids and I tested a variety of cheeses, evaluating the flavor and meltability of each. In the end, we found that pepper Jack cheese, with its hint of spice, provided the best overall flavor.

Unsalted butter, for cooking

8 slices bread, such as rye or wheat

8 (1-ounce) slices pepper Jack cheese

8 ounces thin-sliced deli ham, divided

1 tomato, sliced

1. Butter each bread slice on one side. Arrange the cheese, ham, and tomato slices by the stove for easy assembly.

2. Heat a large skillet over medium heat. Add as many slices of bread (butter-side down) as can comfortably fit in the skillet with space between them (I usually do two at a time) but no more than half the slices. Top each with 1 slice of cheese and one-fourth of the ham, taking care to drape it on the bread. Top the ham with tomato slices and an additional slice of cheese. Close each sandwich with a slice of bread, buttered-side up.

3. Cook for 2 to 3 minutes per side until browned. After flipping the sandwich, press down to compact it. This helps the cheese bring the sandwich together. Continue until all the sandwiches have been made. Halve or quarter the sandwiches and serve immediately.

BUDGET TRICK: Although we love pepper Jack the best, American cheese was a good second best. Feel free to substitute.

PER SERVING: Calories: 381; Total fat: 14g; Sodium: 1,245mg; Carbohydrates: 34g; Fiber: 4g; Sugars: 6g; Protein: 25g.

Hoisin Turkey Lettuce Wraps

SERVES 4 | PREP TIME: 5 MINUTES | COOK TIME: 15 MINUTES

Lettuce wraps have been a thing for as long as I have been cooking, but only in the past few years have I embraced them as something to enjoy at home. I don't know why I waited so long! Warm meat and cool, crisp lettuce are a lovely combination. And, in this case, the richly flavored turkey with hoisin sauce is delightful and satisfying.

1¼ pounds ground turkey

1 bunch scallions, thinly sliced, light parts and dark parts divided

1 tablespoon grated peeled fresh ginger

⅓ cup hoisin sauce

¼ cup water

Sturdy lettuce leaves, such as butter, Bibb, iceberg, or endive (see Budget Trick)

1. Heat a large skillet over medium heat. Add the ground turkey and cook, stirring occasionally to break up the meat, until no longer pink, 6 to 8 minutes.

2. Add the light scallion parts and the ginger and stir well to combine. Cook for 2 to 3 minutes, or until the scallions are softened.

3. Drizzle the hoisin all over the turkey mixture and add the water to the pan. Stir well. Cook for 4 to 6 minutes, until the liquid evaporates. Serve in lettuce leaves, sprinkled with the dark green scallion parts.

BUDGET TRICK: If using butter, Bibb, or iceberg lettuce, you will need 1 head of lettuce to start but will likely have leftovers. Choose whatever lettuce you like that is affordable. I love endive, but it takes about 4 heads ($4 to $6) to accommodate the recipe. A head of iceberg lettuce, however, costs about $2.

PER SERVING: Calories: 314; Total fat: 13g; Sodium: 486mg; Carbohydrates: 15g; Fiber: 3g; Sugars: 9g; Protein: 35g.

Mushroom-Hummus Wraps with Roasted Red Peppers and Artichoke Hearts

SERVES 4 | PREP TIME: 10 MINUTES | COOK TIME: 10 MINUTES

Meaty, warm mushrooms combine with cool hummus, sweet roasted red peppers, and robust marinated artichoke hearts in this tasty, filling wrap. It's filled with so much flavor and is best made fresh and enjoyed immediately.

1 tablespoon olive oil

6 ounces portobello mushrooms, sliced

Salt

Freshly ground black pepper

4 large sandwich wraps

⅓ cup hummus

½ cup roasted red pepper strips

½ cup chopped marinated artichoke hearts

2 cups shredded lettuce

1. In a large skillet over medium heat, heat the olive oil. Add the mushrooms and lightly season with salt and pepper. Cook for 5 to 7 minutes, stirring and turning occasionally, until browned and softened. Remove from the heat.

2. Place the wraps on a work surface or cutting board. Spread the hummus, dividing it evenly, in a line down the center of each wrap, avoiding the edges. Top each with the mushrooms, roasted red pepper strips, artichoke hearts, and lettuce.

3. Fold in the ends of the wrap; then turn and roll it into a cylinder, taking care to tuck in the ends as you go. Secure with toothpicks and halve each wrap for serving.

BUDGET TRICK: Convenience usually comes at a premium, but one exception is sliced mushrooms. They are often the same price as their unsliced counterpart, so don't be afraid to buy the ones that are ready to use and save a little time.

PER SERVING: Calories: 288; Total fat: 12g; Sodium: 553mg; Carbohydrates: 37g; Fiber: 7g; Sugars: 3g; Protein: 9g.

Buffalo Blue Cheese Cauliflower Wraps

SERVES 4 | PREP TIME: 10 MINUTES | COOK TIME: 45 MINUTES

Fans of the zingy flavor of buffalo sauce will adore this vegetarian wrap. Fresh cauliflower is seasoned and roasted to tender perfection and then piled into a wrap with creamy blue cheese. The result is a spicy, fragrant delight.

1 head cauliflower, broken into 1-inch florets

1 tablespoon canola oil

1 tablespoon bread crumbs

Salt

Freshly ground black pepper

⅓ cup buffalo sauce

4 large tortillas

1 cup shredded lettuce

½ cup crumbled blue cheese

1. Preheat the oven to 400°F. Line a baking sheet with aluminum foil.

2. In a large bowl, toss together the cauliflower and canola oil. Sprinkle with the bread crumbs and season with salt and pepper. Toss well. Arrange the cauliflower on the prepared baking sheet.

3. Bake for 20 minutes. Stir well. Bake for 20 to 25 minutes more, until lightly browned.

4. Transfer the cauliflower to a large bowl, add the buffalo sauce, and toss well to coat.

5. Place the tortillas on a work surface or cutting board. Divide the lettuce evenly among the tortillas, and top with 2 tablespoons of blue cheese and one-fourth of the cauliflower. Fold in the ends of the wrap; then turn and roll it into a cylinder, and halve each wrap for serving.

BUDGET TRICK: If cauliflower is on sale, this is a great recipe to double. It reheats well for additional wraps or can be enjoyed as a side dish. You can also freeze cooked cauliflower for 1 to 2 months.

PER SERVING: Calories: 373; Total fat: 14g; Sodium: 1,234mg; Carbohydrates: 49g; Fiber: 6g; Sugars: 3g; Protein: 13g.

Barbecue Roast Beef Wraps

SERVES 4 | PREP TIME: 10 MINUTES | COOK TIME: 5 MINUTES

A little bit crunchy, a little bit sweet, a lot of meaty, cheesy flavor. These easy, flavorful wraps are among my son's very favorite lunches. Best of all, they take minutes to whip up and can even be packed for picnics or in lunchboxes.

4 (6-inch) flour tortillas

¼ cup barbecue sauce

**4 slices
    cheddar cheese**

**½ pound deli roast
    beef, thinly sliced**

**¼ cup red onion,
    very thinly sliced**

**¼ cup green peppers,
    very thinly sliced**

1. Heat a dry skillet over medium heat. Working with one skillet at a time, heat the tortillas for about 15 seconds per side, until just warmed. Transfer to a cutting board.

2. Spread 1 tablespoon of barbecue sauce in a line down the center of each tortilla. Top with a slice of cheddar cheese, ¼ of the roast beef, ¼ of the red onion, and ¼ of the green peppers.

3. Tightly roll the wraps and secure each with two toothpicks. Cut in half.

BUDGET TRICK: **If roast beef is too pricey, deli turkey or chicken, thinly sliced, can be substituted in this recipe.**

PER SERVING: Calories: 282; Total fat: 12g; Sodium: 656mg; Carbohydrates: 22g; Fiber: 2g; Sugars: 6g; Protein: 22g.

Noodles with
Broccoli, Carrots,
and Red Cabbage,
PAGE 64

II

Vegetarian and Vegan Mains

IIIIIIIIIIIIIIIIIIIIIIIIIIIIIIIIIIIIIIIIIIIIIIIIIIIIIIIIIIIIIIIIIIIIIIIIIIIIIIIIIIIIIIIIII

Broccoli-Pesto Pasta

SERVES 4 | PREP TIME: 15 MINUTES | COOK TIME: 10 MINUTES

Traditionally, pesto is made with basil. But when you mix up the flavors, you get a whole different dish. In this case, raw broccoli becomes the base for an earthy, bright, creamy sauce made with walnuts, olive oil, and Parmesan cheese. It's delicious—and so are the leftovers. Be sure to use a Parmesan cheese made with vegetarian rennet to ensure that this is a vegetarian dish.

2 cups packed fresh broccoli florets with chopped and peeled stems

2 garlic cloves, peeled

½ cup walnuts

½ cup grated Parmesan cheese

½ cup olive oil

½ cup water

1 teaspoon salt, plus more for cooking the pasta

1 pound dried pasta of choice

1. In a food processor, combine the broccoli, garlic, walnuts, Parmesan cheese, olive oil, water, and 1 teaspoon salt. Process until smooth, stopping to scrape down the sides as needed. Set aside to allow the flavors to come together while you make the pasta.

2. Bring a large pot of salted water to a boil over high heat. Add the pasta and cook according to the package directions to your desired doneness. Drain, reserving a few ladles of pasta water. Transfer the pasta to a large bowl and add the pesto. Toss well to combine. If needed, add a little pasta water to loosen the sauce. Refrigerate leftovers in an airtight container to enjoy for lunch tomorrow.

BUDGET TRICK: If you aren't that familiar with using broccoli stems, this is a great way to experiment with them and reduce food waste. The sauce could even be made with all stems if you prefer.

PER SERVING: Calories: 775; Total fat: 41g; Sodium: 845mg; Carbohydrates: 87g; Fiber: 12g; Sugars: 3g; Protein: 22g.

5 INGREDIENTS | DAIRY-FREE | GLUTEN-FREE | NUT-FREE | ONE POT | VEGAN

Scallion and Chickpea Rice Casserole

SERVES 4 | PREP TIME: 10 MINUTES | COOK TIME: 45 MINUTES

Delicately flavored with the oniony fragrance of scallion and earthiness of rosemary, this easy dinner is perfect for rice lovers. The great thing about casseroles like this is they are so simple to prepare—mix the ingredients, bake, and they come out of the oven perfectly cooked and ready to serve. It's a fantastic, hands-off way to get dinner on the table.

1 cup raw long-grain white rice

2 cups Veggie Scraps Vegetable Stock (page 138) or store-bought vegetable broth

1 bunch scallions, thinly sliced

1 (15.5-ounce) can chickpeas, drained and rinsed

1 teaspoon dried rosemary

1 teaspoon salt

¼ teaspoon freshly ground black pepper

1. Preheat the oven to 350°F.

2. In a 9-by-13-inch glass baking dish, stir together the rice, vegetable stock, scallions, chickpeas, rosemary, salt, and pepper.

3. Bake for 40 to 45 minutes, until the rice is cooked through. Stir and serve immediately.

BUDGET TRICK: **Although this recipe calls for canned chickpeas, dried chickpeas work, too—and can be even more budget-friendly. Substitute 1⅓ cups cooked dried chickpeas for the canned and complete the recipe as directed.**

PER SERVING: Calories: 289; Total fat: 1g; Sodium: 717mg; Carbohydrates: 60g; Fiber: 7g; Sugars: 1g; Protein: 10g.

Chipotle, Sweet Potato, and Black Bean Enchilada Casserole

SERVES 4 | PREP TIME: 15 MINUTES | COOK TIME: 45 MINUTES

My family loves enchiladas, but I don't always have time to make them in the traditional rolled way. This casserole combines all the flavors of enchiladas in an easy, layered dish. These are excellent served with an array of toppings like diced avocado, tomato, and sour cream. But be warned: These can be a bit spicy. Halve the amount of chipotle pepper for a less spicy version.

1 large (12- to 16-ounce) sweet potato, cut into ½-inch dice

Nonstick cooking spray

1 (15.5-ounce) can black beans, drained and rinsed

1 tablespoon unsalted butter

1 tablespoon all-purpose flour

2 cups Veggie Scraps Vegetable Stock (page 138) or store-bought vegetable broth

1 teaspoon ground cumin

1 teaspoon garlic powder

1 canned chipotle pepper in adobo sauce

1. Bring a medium pot of water to a boil over high heat. Add the sweet potato and boil for 15 to 18 minutes, until tender. Drain thoroughly.

2. Preheat the oven to 400°F. Coat an 8-by-8-inch glass baking dish with nonstick cooking spray. Set aside.

3. In a medium bowl, stir together the sweet potato and black beans. Set aside.

4. In a small saucepan over medium heat, melt the butter. Whisk in the flour and cook for 1 to 2 minutes, until fully combined and golden in color. Don't cook it too long before adding the stock or it will begin to burn.

5. A little at a time, whisk in the vegetable stock until combined. Stir in the cumin, garlic powder, chipotle pepper, adobo sauce, and a pinch of salt and pepper. Cook for 3 to 4 minutes, stirring occasionally, until thickened. Remove from the heat.

1 teaspoon adobo
  sauce (from the can)

Salt

Freshly ground
  black pepper

8 (6-inch) corn tortillas

1 cup shredded
  Cheddar cheese

6. Add 1 cup of the sauce to the sweet potatoes and black beans and stir to combine. Spread the mixture in the prepared baking dish. Top with the corn tortillas, overlapping them to fit. Pour the remaining sauce over the tortillas, soaking them all. Sprinkle the Cheddar cheese on top.

7. Bake for 15 to 20 minutes until the cheese is melted and the dish is bubbling at the edges. Let cool for 5 minutes before serving.

BUDGET TRICK: Corn tortillas are an economical ingredient, and you won't use them all with this dish. Refrigerate leftovers for taco night (warm them in a dry, hot skillet for about 10 seconds per side before using). If you will use the remaining chipotle peppers within 2 weeks, refrigerate them in an airtight container with the sauce. If you want to save them for later use, freeze them in an airtight container for up to 4 months. If freezing, leave space in the container for expansion as the sauce freezes.

PER SERVING: Calories: 439; Total fat: 15g; Sodium: 400mg; Carbohydrates: 62g; Fiber: 13g; Sugars: 4g; Protein: 18g.

Gnocchi with Sautéed Tomatoes and Spinach

SERVES 4 | PREP TIME: 10 MINUTES | COOK TIME: 15 MINUTES

In this dish, the pillowy texture of gnocchi is complemented by bright, juicy burst tomatoes, zesty garlic, and earthy spinach. Easy to make and full of flavor, this dinner is a great solution for the busiest nights.

1 (16-ounce) package dried gnocchi

2 tablespoons olive oil

1 pint grape tomatoes

3 garlic cloves, minced

2 cups frozen chopped spinach

Salt

Freshly ground black pepper

1. Bring a large pot of water to a boil over high heat. Add the gnocchi and cook according to package directions. Drain.

2. Meanwhile, in a skillet over medium heat, heat the olive oil. Add the tomatoes and cook for 7 to 8 minutes, shaking the pan occasionally, until they begin to burst. Stir in the garlic and cook for 1 minute more or until fragrant.

3. Stir in the spinach and season with salt and pepper. Cook for 3 to 4 minutes, stirring, until the spinach is thawed.

4. Add the cooked gnocchi to the skillet and toss to combine. Taste and season with more salt and pepper as needed.

> **BUDGET TRICK:** The flavor of olive oil adds to dishes like this in a way other oils can't. But olive oil can be pricey. Look outside the grocery store for good, less expensive sources such as discount retailers selling items that didn't sell elsewhere.

PER SERVING: Calories: 316; Total fat: 9g; Sodium: 70mg; Carbohydrates: 50g; Fiber: 6g; Sugars: 3g; Protein: 11g.

Chickpea-Pumpkin Coconut Curry

SERVES 4 | PREP TIME: 15 MINUTES | COOK TIME: 35 MINUTES

Thai red curry has a sweet heat thanks to the combination of spicy red curry, creamy coconut milk, and a touch of brown sugar. In this version, it's made even richer with the addition of pumpkin and sweet potato. Carrot, onion, chickpeas, and more make this comforting dish a hearty dinner success.

1 tablespoon olive oil

1 yellow onion, diced

2 carrots, cut into coins

1 sweet potato, diced

3 garlic cloves, minced

1 (15-ounce) can pumpkin puree

1 (15.5-ounce) can chickpeas, drained and rinsed

2 tablespoons red curry paste

1 tablespoon light brown sugar

1 (13.5-ounce) can coconut milk

1 cup water

¼ cup chopped fresh cilantro

1. In a large skillet over medium heat, heat the olive oil. Add the onion, carrots, and sweet potato. Cook for about 10 minutes, stirring, until the onion begins to soften and brown. Stir in the garlic and cook for about 1 minute or until fragrant.

2. Stir in the pumpkin, chickpeas, red curry paste, and brown sugar until well combined. Cook for 2 to 3 minutes, stirring, until steamy.

3. Stir in the coconut milk and water. Reduce the heat to medium-low, cover the skillet, and simmer for 15 to 20 minutes, stirring occasionally. The vegetables should be cooked through, and the sauce should be thoroughly combined. Remove from heat and stir in the cilantro before serving.

BUDGET TRICK: Although pumpkin puree is available year-round, it's usually sold at sale prices in late October and November. Stock your pantry then, taking care to check expiration dates.

PER SERVING: Calories: 428; Total fat: 23g; Sodium: 377mg; Carbohydrates: 49g; Fiber: 11g; Sugars: 12g; Protein: 9g.

Noodles with Broccoli, Carrots, and Red Cabbage

SERVES 4 | PREP TIME: 15 MINUTES | COOK TIME: 15 MINUTES

You can use whatever noodle you happen to have on hand for this dish: Soba, somen, udon, ramen or even spaghetti will all work fine. Despite the touch of sriracha in this recipe, these noodles aren't spicy. It adds a hint of spice that's offset by the other flavors.

1 tablespoon canola oil

3 cups bite-size broccoli florets with chopped and peeled stems

1 cup julienned carrot

2 cups thinly shredded red cabbage

1 (9.5-ounce) package dried noodles

3 tablespoons soy sauce

2 tablespoons water

1 tablespoon rice vinegar

1 tablespoon light brown sugar

1 teaspoon sriracha

1 teaspoon grated peeled fresh ginger

¼ cup chopped fresh cilantro

1. In a large skillet over medium heat, heat the canola oil until hot. Add the broccoli, carrot, and red cabbage. Sauté for 8 to 10 minutes, stirring occasionally, until tender.

2. Meanwhile, bring a large pot of water to a boil over high heat. Add the soba noodles and cook according to the package directions. Drain.

3. In a small bowl, whisk the soy sauce, water, vinegar, brown sugar, sriracha, and ginger to combine.

4. In a large bowl, combine the sautéed vegetables, cooked soba noodles, and sauce. Toss to coat. Garnish with cilantro.

BUDGET TRICK: Most people throw away broccoli stems, but really they are delicious and not to be wasted. Trim the ends of the stems, peel them, and dice them, and they can be used in pretty much any recipe that calls for broccoli.

PER SERVING: Calories: 324; Total fat: 4g; Sodium: 1,285mg; Carbohydrates: 64g; Fiber: 3g; Sugars: 8g; Protein: 12g.

If you don't have
fresh broccoli, frozen
will work, too!

Baked Potatoes with Caramelized Onions and Brussels Sprouts

SERVES 4 | PREP TIME: 10 MINUTES | COOK TIME: 1 HOUR

The hearty baked potato is a blank canvas for toppings. In this version, a combination of sweet caramelized red onion and tender Brussels sprouts adds a confetti of flavor to the humble potato. This is also highly customizable. Drizzle a little balsamic vinegar on top, pile on some microgreens, or sprinkle with your favorite cheese. There are so many ways to make this dish your own.

4 baking potatoes, such as Yukon Gold, rinsed in cool water and pricked a few times on the top with a fork

1 tablespoon olive oil

1 large red onion, quartered and sliced

Salt

Freshly ground black pepper

1 pound Brussels sprouts, trimmed and sliced

1. Position the oven racks so the top rack is in the middle and the lower rack is just below it. Place a baking sheet on the lower rack. Preheat the oven to 400°F.

2. Place the potatoes on the upper rack, pricked-side up.

3. Bake for 45 to 55 minutes, until tender.

4. Meanwhile, in a large skillet over medium heat, heat the olive oil. Add the red onion and lightly season with salt and pepper. Cook for 10 to 12 minutes, stirring occasionally, until the onion begins to brown.

5. Add the Brussels sprouts to the skillet and cook, stirring, for about 10 minutes or until tender. Taste and season with more salt and pepper as needed.

6. Remove the baked potatoes from the oven and cut a T in the top of each, squeezing the potatoes to open them. Divide the onion and Brussels sprout mixture evenly among the potatoes to serve.

PER SERVING: Calories: 193; Total fat: 4g; Sodium: 30mg; Carbohydrates: 39g; Fiber: 8g; Sugars: 7g; Protein: 8g.

GLUTEN-FREE | NUT-FREE | VEGETARIAN

Spinach and Tomato Frittata with Feta

SERVES 8 | PREP TIME: 15 MINUTES | COOK TIME: 30 MINUTES

Sure, this recipe sounds fancy. But frittatas are super easy to make, and are incredibly budget-friendly. In this version, sweet, juicy tomatoes and salty, rich feta top off this hearty dish. And leftovers are great, too.

12 large eggs

1 (5.3-ounce) container plain Greek yogurt, drained

2 garlic cloves, minced

1 cup frozen chopped spinach, broken up

½ teaspoon onion powder

½ teaspoon paprika

½ teaspoon dried rosemary

1 teaspoon salt

½ teaspoon freshly ground black pepper

2 tablespoons olive oil

1 cup halved cherry tomatoes

½ cup crumbled feta cheese

1. Preheat the oven to 350°F.

2. In a large bowl, whisk the eggs, yogurt, garlic, spinach, onion powder, paprika, rosemary, salt, and pepper until just combined.

3. In a large oven-safe skillet (cast iron recommended) over medium-high heat, heat the olive oil. Add the egg mixture and cook, without disturbing, for about 5 minutes until the sides and bottom begin to firm.

4. Top the frittata with the tomatoes, cut-side up, taking care to distribute them evenly. Sprinkle with the feta cheese.

5. Bake for 20 to 25 minutes until the top is just beginning to brown. Let cool for 5 minutes before cutting it into 8 wedges and serving.

6. Refrigerate any leftovers in an airtight container for up to 5 days.

BUDGET TRICK: **You might not think of the dollar store for groceries, but some sell nonperishables like spices.**

PER SERVING: Calories: 195; Total fat: 14g; Sodium: 528mg; Carbohydrates: 5g; Fiber: 1g; Sugars: 2g; Protein: 13g.

Garlicky White Bean Burgers

SERVES 4 | PREP TIME: 10 MINUTES | COOK TIME: 15 MINUTES

Crunchy on the outside, soft on the inside—these burgers are a treat. But don't expect a meat look-alike. Instead, appreciate this burger for what it is: a delightful bean burger with lots of flavor. And the toppings make this extra tasty.

1 (15.5-ounce) can cannellini beans, drained and rinsed

⅓ cup Italian bread crumbs

3 garlic cloves, crushed and chopped

1 scallion, chopped

1 large egg

1 teaspoon salt

½ teaspoon freshly ground black pepper

2 tablespoons olive oil

4 hamburger buns

1 avocado, peeled, halved, pitted, and sliced

4 slices red onion

1 tomato, sliced

Lettuce leaves, for serving

1. In a food processor or blender, combine the beans, bread crumbs, garlic, scallion, egg, salt, and pepper. Process until smooth.

2. In a skillet over medium heat, heat the olive oil. Drop the bean mixture in by the spoonful, creating 4 rounds. Using the spoon, press the rounds into patty shapes. Cook for 6 to 8 minutes per side until golden, flipping once. Remove from the skillet.

3. Arrange the hamburger buns on each of 4 plates. Top each bun with a white bean patty, avocado slices, red onion, tomato, and lettuce.

BUDGET TRICK: When planning meals for the week, remember that hamburger buns come in packages of eight. For a low-waste plan for four people, plan two dinners using them.

PER SERVING: Calories: 427; Total fat: 20g; Sodium: 1,059mg; Carbohydrates: 52g; Fiber: 10g; Sugars: 5g; Protein: 13g.

Ravioli with Asparagus and Brown Butter

SERVES 4 | PREP TIME: 5 MINUTES | COOK TIME: 15 MINUTES

When cooked until it begins to brown, butter's flavor deepens until almost nutty. In this dish, brown butter coats tender cheese ravioli and perfectly cooked asparagus for a lovely, light meal. Serve this with a salad.

1 (24-ounce) package cheese ravioli

1 tablespoon olive oil

1 pound asparagus, woody ends trimmed, cut into 1-inch pieces

1 tablespoon unsalted butter

Salt

Freshly ground black pepper

1. Bring a large pot of water to a boil over high heat. Add the ravioli and cook according to the package directions. Drain and return to the pot. Set aside.

2. Meanwhile, in a large skillet over medium heat, heat the olive oil. Add the asparagus and cook for 7 to 8 minutes, stirring occasionally, until browned.

3. Add the butter and let melt without disturbing. Continue cooking for 1 to 2 minutes more, watching it carefully to prevent burning, until the butter begins to brown and smells nutty. Once the color begins to change, remove it from the heat. Immediately pour the asparagus and butter mixture over the ravioli. Season with salt and pepper and gently stir to coat.

BUDGET TRICK: Fresh asparagus is best for this recipe. However, if it's expensive or out of season, try frozen asparagus instead.

PER SERVING: Calories: 392; Total fat: 19g; Sodium: 543mg; Carbohydrates: 42g; Fiber: 8g; Sugars: 4g; Protein: 20g.

Garlic-Ginger Mushroom Bowls with Scallions

SERVES 4 | PREP TIME: 10 MINUTES | COOK TIME: 20 MINUTES

The rich flavors of garlic, ginger, and soy sauce give the well-cooked mushrooms in this dish tremendous flavor. Combined with meaty edamame and bright scallions, it's a tasty treat. To make this gluten-free, substitute tamari for the soy sauce.

1 cup raw white rice

1 tablespoon olive oil

1 pound cremini mushrooms, sliced

Salt

Freshly ground black pepper

1 bunch scallions, sliced, whites and greens separated

½ cup shelled edamame

2 garlic cloves, minced

1 tablespoon grated peeled fresh ginger

1 tablespoon soy sauce

1. Cook the white rice according to the package directions.

2. Once the rice is nearly ready, in a large skillet over medium heat, heat the olive oil. Add the mushrooms and lightly season with salt and pepper. Cook for 10 to 12 minutes, stirring, until browned and soft. Add the scallion whites and sauté for 2 to 3 minutes, until softened.

3. Stir in the edamame, garlic, ginger, and soy sauce until combined. Cook for 3 to 4 minutes, stirring, until the liquid is absorbed and the edamame are hot.

4. Divide the rice evenly among 4 bowls. Top each with one-fourth of the mushroom mixture and sprinkle with the scallion greens.

BUDGET TRICK: When buying ingredients like soy sauce, consider purchasing a larger bottle, which will last longer and save you money over time.

PER SERVING: Calories: 262; Total fat: 5g; Sodium: 254mg; Carbohydrates: 46g; Fiber: 3g; Sugars: 3g; Protein: 10g.

Lemon-Garlic Orzo with Peas and White Beans

SERVES 4 | PREP TIME: 10 MINUTES | COOK TIME: 10 MINUTES

Over the summer, my kids and I grow tomatoes, root vegetables, and more. Last summer we added peas to the mix—our harvest was hearty, and we froze plenty for winter. Homegrown or store-bought, the bright, summery flavor of peas brings this dish alive. And the zesty lemon-garlic combination is a wonderful complement.

8 ounces dried orzo

1 cup frozen peas

1 (15.5-ounce) can white beans, drained and rinsed

1 tablespoon olive oil

1 tablespoon unsalted butter

1 scallion, sliced, whites and greens separated

3 garlic cloves, minced

Juice of 1 lemon

Grated zest of 1 lemon

Salt

Freshly ground black pepper

1. Bring a large pot of water to a boil over high heat. Add the orzo and cook according to the package directions. When about 3 minutes remain until the orzo will be done, add the peas to the pot for the remaining cook time. Drain and return to the pot. Stir in the white beans.

2. In a large skillet over medium heat, add the olive oil and butter to melt. Add the scallion whites and garlic. Cook for about 2 minutes, stirring, until the scallion has softened.

3. Stir in the lemon juice. Bring to a boil and cook for 1 minute. Pour the sauce over the orzo mixture.

4. Sprinkle with the lemon zest and the scallion greens. Toss well to combine. Taste and season with salt and pepper as needed.

BUDGET TRICK: Did you know butter can be frozen? It often goes on sale near the holiday season, so stock up and freeze it.

PER SERVING: Calories: 379; Total fat: 8g; Sodium: 142mg; Carbohydrates: 65g; Fiber: 10g; Sugars: 3g; Protein: 14g.

Tomato-Basil Risotto

SERVES 4 | PREP TIME: 10 MINUTES | COOK TIME: 55 MINUTES

Risotto is my go-to comfort food. Creamy, hearty, and tasty, I love eating it. But more than that, I love making it. The slow process forces you to stop, be in the moment, and pay attention—all good things. In this version, tomato permeates all the grains of rice, as it's part of the liquid added to make the dish. Be sure to use a cheese made with vegetarian rennet to ensure that this is a vegetarian dish.

1 (14.5-ounce) can diced tomatoes

2 tablespoons dried basil

4 cups Veggie Scraps Vegetable Stock (page 138) or store-bought vegetable broth

1 tablespoon olive oil

1 onion, diced

1 cup raw Arborio rice

½ cup white wine or more stock (know that not using wine will change the final flavor of the dish)

½ cup grated Parmesan or other hard cheese

Salt

Freshly ground black pepper

1. In a blender, combine the tomatoes and their juices, basil, and 1 cup of vegetable stock. Puree until smooth. Add the remaining vegetable stock and pulse to combine.

2. In a large pot over medium heat, heat the olive oil. Add the onion and cook for 10 to 12 minutes, stirring occasionally, until it begins to brown.

3. Add the rice and stir to combine. Cook for 1 minute. Stir in the white wine and cook until the liquid is absorbed, 2 to 3 minutes.

4. Begin adding the tomato mixture to the rice using this process: Add about ½ cup, stir, let it cook until it absorbs into the rice, and then add more. Continue, taking your time to add the tomato stock about ½ cup at a time and stirring frequently, until all the liquid has been added. This should take 35 to 40 minutes.

5. Remove from the heat and stir in the Parmesan cheese. Taste and season with salt and pepper as needed.

PER SERVING: Calories: 319; Total fat: 8g; Sodium: 442mg; Carbohydrates: 11g; Fiber: 4g; Sugars: 4g; Protein: 11g.

Vegan Bolognese

SERVES 4 | PREP TIME: 10 MINUTES | COOK TIME: 45 MINUTES

In a traditional Bolognese sauce, onion and meat are simmered together to make a hearty pasta sauce. In this version, vegetables and lentils take the place of the meat to create a hearty, filling sauce that satisfies. This was the surprise hit of recipe testing while creating this cookbook.

1 teaspoon salt, plus more for cooking the pasta

8 ounces dried pasta of choice

1 tablespoon olive oil

1 onion, diced

1 red bell pepper, diced

1 celery stalk, diced

3 garlic cloves, minced

1 (28-ounce) can crushed tomatoes

1 (15.5-ounce) can diced tomatoes and their juices

2 tablespoons dried basil

½ cup dried brown lentils

1 cup water

1. Bring a large pot of salted water to a boil over high heat. Add the pasta and cook according to the package directions. Drain and set aside.

2. While the pasta cooks, in another large pot over medium heat, heat the olive oil. Add the onion, red bell pepper, and celery. Cook for 10 to 12 minutes, stirring occasionally, until softened. Stir in the garlic and cook for 1 minute or until fragrant.

3. Stir in the crushed tomatoes, diced tomatoes and their juices, basil, and 1 teaspoon salt.

4. Stir in the lentils and water. Cover the pot and reduce the heat to medium-low. Simmer for 20 to 30 minutes, until the lentils are softened. Serve the sauce over the cooked pasta.

BUDGET TRICK: Save any extra sauce. It can be portioned into freezer-safe containers and frozen for up to 4 months.

PER SERVING: Calories: 391; Total fat: 5g; Sodium: 1,050mg; Carbohydrates: 72g; Fiber: 13g; Sugars: 10g; Protein: 22g.

Lemon-Caper Fish Tacos
with Blistered Tomatoes
and Avocado,
PAGE 76

||||||||||||||||||||||||||||||||||||||||||||||||||||||||||||||||||||||||||||||||||||||||||||||||||

CHAPTER SIX

Poultry and Seafood Mains

||||||||||||||||||||||||||||||||||||||||||||||||||||||||||||||||||||||||||||||||||||||||||||||||||

Lemon-Caper Fish Tacos with Blistered Tomatoes and Avocado

SERVES 4 | PREP TIME: 10 MINUTES | COOK TIME: 20 MINUTES

On a rare afternoon when just my son and I were home, I whipped up a batch of these fish tacos for lunch. When you plate these tacos, they feel special, yet they are easy to make and cook quickly. What makes them so exquisite are the warm, blistered tomatoes combined with lemon zest and capers topping the fish. *Yum.* If you really love avocado, it's totally okay to double the amount.

Nonstick cooking spray

1 pound halibut fillets

1 pint grape tomatoes, or cherry tomatoes

Salt

Freshly ground black pepper

12 (6-inch) corn tortillas

1 lemon

2 tablespoons capers, drained

1 avocado, peeled, halved, pitted, and sliced

1. Preheat the oven to 400°F. Line a large baking sheet with aluminum foil and coat it with nonstick cooking spray.

2. Arrange the halibut fillets on one side of the baking sheet. Pile the tomatoes on the other side. Spray all with nonstick cooking spray and season with salt and pepper.

3. Bake for 12 to 16 minutes, until the tomatoes burst and the fillets are opaque in color.

4. When the tomatoes and fish are done, in a dry skillet over medium heat, warm the tortillas for about 10 seconds per side. Arrange 3 tortillas on each of 4 plates.

5. Using a fork, break the halibut into large (about 1-inch) chunks. Divide the halibut evenly among the tortillas. Top each with tomatoes.

6. Zest the lemon over all the tacos. Cut the lemon into 8 wedges. Set aside.

7. Sprinkle the capers on the tacos and finish with avocado slices. Serve each plate with 2 lemon wedges for squeezing.

BUDGET TRICK: **If halibut is pricey, other firm white fish such as cod, flounder, or sole can be used interchangeably in this recipe.**

PER SERVING: Calories: 423; Total fat: 13g; Sodium: 252mg; Carbohydrates: 45g; Fiber: 10g; Sugars: 3g; Protein: 37g.

Orange-Thyme Roast Chicken

**SERVES 4 | PREP TIME: 10 MINUTES | COOK TIME: 1 HOUR 15 MINUTES |
RESTING TIME: 15 MINUTES**

The great thing about making a whole chicken is it will feed you for more than one meal, and leftovers can be used in other dishes. In this version, a pleasant citrus-based rub gives the chicken lots of flavor.

Grated zest of 1 orange

1 teaspoon dried thyme

2 garlic cloves, minced

1 (3- to 4-pound) roasting chicken

Nonstick cooking spray

Salt

Freshly ground black pepper

1. Preheat the oven to 450°F. Line a baking sheet with aluminum foil and place a wire rack on top.

2. In a small bowl, stir together the orange zest, thyme, and garlic. Set aside.

3. Place the chicken, breast-side up, on the rack. Using your fingers, gently loosen the skin on the chicken. Spread the orange mixture underneath the skin all over the chicken, taking care to distribute it as evenly as you can.

4. Spray the chicken with nonstick cooking spray. Season the outside with salt and pepper.

5. Bake for 20 minutes. Reduce the oven temperature to 375°F and bake for 45 to 55 minutes more, or until the chicken reaches an internal temperature of 165°F and the juices run clear. Let sit for 15 minutes before carving.

6. Refrigerate any leftovers in an airtight container for 4 to 5 days.

BUDGET TRICK: Once you've cut up the chicken, don't discard the carcass! It's perfect for making Slow Cooker Chicken Stock (page 136). Refrigerate the carcass in a resealable bag or airtight container for 4 to 5 days, or freeze for up to 2 months. (I prefer to use the carcass for stock immediately.) Also, save the zested orange and make Zesty Orange-Thyme Vinaigrette (page 141) for tossing on salads this week.

PER SERVING: Calories: 217; Total fat: 15g; Sodium: 654mg; Carbohydrates: 2g; Fiber: <1g; Sugars: 1g; Protein: 22g.

Sheet Pan Garlic Salmon with Roasted Snap Peas

SERVES 4 | PREP TIME: 10 MINUTES | COOK TIME: 20 MINUTES

Salmon is the most frequently eaten seafood in our household. Not only do we love it, but it's rich with healthy omega-3 fatty acids, so I can feel good about serving it to my kids. In this sheet pan version, the salmon gets a hearty boost of flavor from garlic. Plus, roasting the snap peas renders them tender while celebrating their natural sweetness. Delightful!

1 pound fresh salmon

1 tablespoon olive oil

2 garlic cloves, minced

Salt

Freshly ground black pepper

2 cups sugar snap peas, rinsed

Nonstick cooking spray

1. Preheat the oven to 400°F. Line a baking sheet with aluminum foil.

2. Arrange the salmon on one side of the prepared baking sheet. Brush with the olive oil and sprinkle evenly with the garlic. Season with salt and pepper.

3. Pile the sugar snap peas on the other side of the baking sheet. Spray the peas with nonstick cooking spray and season with salt and pepper.

4. Bake for 15 to 18 minutes, until the salmon is fork-tender but not overcooked. (When flaked with a fork, it should be juicy, not dried, inside.) Stir the sugar snap peas. Cut the salmon into 4 pieces and serve immediately.

BUDGET TRICK: **When fresh salmon is on sale, it's the ideal ingredient for this dish. But if not, check the freezer section for frozen salmon fillets. They can be a cost-effective way to enjoy salmon.**

PER SERVING: Calories: 231; Total fat: 9g; Sodium: 98mg; Carbohydrates: 6g; Fiber: 2g; Sugars: 2g; Protein: 31g.

Sheet Pan Teriyaki Shrimp with Broccoli

SERVES 4 | PREP TIME: 10 MINUTES | COOK TIME: 35 MINUTES

Shrimp and broccoli make a perfect match in this sweet, hearty dish flavored with teriyaki. I love to serve this on a bed of cooked rice.

4 cups broccoli florets and chopped peeled stems

1 yellow onion, diced

3 garlic cloves, minced

½ cup teriyaki sauce, divided

1 tablespoon olive oil

1 pound shrimp, peeled and deveined

1. Preheat the oven to 400°F. Line a baking sheet with parchment paper. Set aside.

2. In a large bowl, toss together the broccoli, onion, garlic, ¼ cup of teriyaki sauce, and olive oil. Spread the vegetables on the prepared baking sheet.

3. Roast for 20 to 25 minutes, until the broccoli is fork-tender.

4. Meanwhile, in a medium bowl, toss the shrimp with 2 tablespoons of teriyaki sauce. Let sit until the broccoli is done. Pour the shrimp and teriyaki sauce onto the baking sheet and toss to combine with the broccoli mixture.

5. Roast for 5 to 6 minutes more, until the shrimp are opaque and pink.

6. Drizzle with the remaining 2 tablespoons of teriyaki sauce and toss to combine.

BUDGET TRICK: Teriyaki sauce has a long shelf life in the refrigerator. Don't be afraid to buy a large, more economical bottle. It will keep.

PER SERVING: Calories: 224; Total fat: 6g; Sodium: 1,409mg; Carbohydrates: 12g; Fiber: 3g; Sugars: 7g; Protein: 27g.

Slow Cooker Pulled Turkey Tenderloin with Parsley Pesto $ $

SERVES 6 | PREP TIME: 10 MINUTES | COOK TIME: 4 HOURS

You've had pulled pork, maybe brisket, and possibly even pulled chicken. Why not pulled turkey? This easy slow cooker recipe renders the turkey perfect for pulling, and the brightly flavored parsley pesto on top adds a burst of fresh flavor.

FOR THE TENDERLOIN

1¾ to 2 pounds
   turkey tenderloin

½ teaspoon paprika

½ teaspoon salt

¼ teaspoon freshly
   ground black pepper

½ cup white wine, or
   Slow Cooker Chicken
   Stock (page 136),
   or store-bought
   chicken broth

FOR THE PESTO

1 cup fresh parsley

¼ cup
   chopped walnuts

¼ cup freshly grated
   Romano cheese

1 garlic clove, peeled

½ teaspoon salt

¼ cup olive oil

TO MAKE THE TENDERLOIN

1. Place the turkey tenderloin in a slow cooker.

2. In a small bowl, stir together the paprika, salt, and pepper. Spread the spices all over the tenderloin, turning to coat it thoroughly. Pour the wine into the cooker, being careful not to pour it directly on the turkey.

3. Cover the cooker and cook on low heat for 3 to 4 hours, until the turkey reaches an internal temperature of 165°F and can be easily pulled apart using two forks. Remove the turkey from the slow cooker. Let sit for 10 minutes and then shred it with the forks.

TO MAKE THE PESTO

4. In a food processor or blender, combine the parsley, walnuts, Romano cheese, garlic, and salt. Process until thoroughly chopped.

5. Pour in the olive oil and pulse to combine. Drizzle the pesto atop the turkey to serve.

PER SERVING: Calories: 290; Total fat: 15g; Sodium: 544mg; Carbohydrates: 2g; Fiber: 1g; Sugars: <1g; Protein: 36g.

Barbecue Turkey Burgers with Avocado, Roasted Red Pepper, Red Onion, and Tomato

SERVES 4 | PREP TIME: 10 MINUTES | COOK TIME: 15 MINUTES

Seasoning meat before forming it into patties is the key to getting more flavor from your ordinary burgers, but we all know the toppings really *make* the burger. Barbecue sauce, veggies, and more make these burgers a special treat beyond ordinary.

1¼ pounds ground turkey

1 teaspoon paprika

1 teaspoon salt

½ teaspoon freshly ground black pepper

4 hamburger buns

¼ cup barbecue sauce

1 avocado, peeled, halved, pitted, and sliced

½ cup sliced roasted red pepper

4 slices red onion

1 tomato, sliced

1. In a large bowl, mix the ground turkey, paprika, salt, and pepper to combine. Form the meat mixture into 4 equal patties about ¼ inch thick.

2. Heat a large skillet over medium heat. Add the patties. Cook for 12 to 15 minutes, flipping once about halfway through the cooking time, or until cooked through and golden brown.

3. Arrange the hamburger buns on 4 plates. Top each with a turkey patty and 1 tablespoon of barbecue sauce. Arrange avocado slices, roasted red pepper, 1 red onion slice, and tomato slices on each.

BUDGET TRICK: Sometimes ground turkey is sold in already-formed patties. It's okay to substitute those when they are on sale and just sprinkle the burgers with the seasonings.

PER SERVING: Calories: 474; Total fat: 22g; Sodium: 1,126mg; Carbohydrates: 33g; Fiber: 4g; Sugars: 11g; Protein: 39g.

Pasta with Lemon-Parsley Clam Sauce

SERVES 4 | PREP TIME: 10 MINUTES | COOK TIME: 15 MINUTES

Clam lovers will enjoy this light, fragrant sauce tossed with angel hair pasta. And you'll enjoy how quick and easy it is to make. Plus, it looks fancy without being expensive or time-consuming to make. Score!

8 ounces dried angel hair pasta

2 tablespoons olive oil

2 garlic cloves, minced

Pinch red pepper flakes

1 (6.5-ounce) can chopped clams in clam juice

¼ cup white wine

¼ cup freshly squeezed lemon juice

½ cup finely minced fresh parsley

Salt

Freshly ground black pepper

1. Bring a large pot of water to a boil over high heat. Add the pasta and cook according to the package directions. Drain.

2. Meanwhile, in a large skillet over medium heat, heat the olive oil. Add the garlic and cook for 1 minute or until fragrant.

3. Stir in the red pepper flakes, clams with their juices, white wine, and lemon juice. Bring to a boil and cook for about 3 minutes to allow the flavors to combine. Remove from the heat. Add the pasta and parsley. Toss well to combine. Taste and season with salt and pepper as needed.

BUDGET TRICK: Have extra parsley? Stick it in the food processor or blender with some water and chop it finely. Then pour it into an ice cube mold and freeze. The parsley cubes can be added to all sorts of dishes.

PER SERVING: Calories: 309; Total fat: 8g; Sodium: 265mg; Carbohydrates: 46g; Fiber: 2g; Sugars: 3g; Protein: 11g.

Breaded Turkey with Tomato-Parsley Orzo

SERVES 4 | PREP TIME: 10 MINUTES | COOK TIME: 25 MINUTES

Crispy, well-seasoned turkey cutlets are lovely served with tender, gently flavored orzo. This easy dish is a warming comfort on a cold day.

2 tablespoons
all-purpose flour

1 large egg, beaten

½ cup bread crumbs

4 (4-ounce)
turkey cutlets

2 tablespoons olive oil

8 ounces dried orzo

1 tomato, diced

⅓ cup finely chopped
fresh parsley

Pinch red
pepper flakes

Salt

Freshly ground
black pepper

1. Place the flour on a rimmed plate or in a shallow bowl. Place the egg in a second rimmed plate or shallow bowl and the bread crumbs in a third. Dredge the turkey cutlets in the flour, egg, and then bread crumbs, coating both sides in each.

2. In a large skillet over medium heat, heat the olive oil. Add the breaded turkey cutlets and cook for 15 to 20 minutes, flipping once about halfway through the cooking time, until golden brown and cooked through. They're done when they reach an internal temperature of 165°F and the juices run clear.

3. Meanwhile, bring a medium pot of water to a boil over high heat. Add the orzo and cook according to the package directions. Drain and transfer to a large bowl. Add the tomato, parsley, and red pepper flakes. Season with salt and pepper and toss to combine.

4. Divide the orzo evenly among 4 plates and top with a turkey cutlet.

PER SERVING: Calories: 470; Total fat: 10g; Sodium: 99mg; Carbohydrates: 56g; Fiber: 3g; Sugars: 3g; Protein: 39g.

Buffalo Chicken and Broccoli Rice Bowls with Blue Cheese

SERVES 4 | PREP TIME: 10 MINUTES | COOK TIME: 25 MINUTES

The broccoli and lightly breaded chicken in this dish really soak up the buffalo sauce—and it's delicious! I especially love the layers of flavors and textures in these rice bowls. Use the best blue cheese you can afford—it makes it all the better.

1 cup raw long-grain rice

1 pound boneless, skinless chicken breast, cut into 1-inch pieces

½ cup panko bread crumbs

Salt

Freshly ground black pepper

2 tablespoons olive oil

3 cups broccoli florets and chopped peeled stems

1 cup buffalo sauce

½ cup crumbled blue cheese

1. Cook the rice according to the package directions.

2. Meanwhile, in a large bowl, combine the chicken and panko bread crumbs. Lightly season with salt and pepper. Stir well to combine and coat the chicken.

3. In a large skillet over medium heat, heat the olive oil. Add the chicken to the skillet and cook for 8 to 10 minutes, stirring occasionally, until opaque.

4. Add the broccoli to the skillet and stir to combine. Cover the skillet and cook for 8 to 10 minutes more, stirring occasionally, until the broccoli is tender and the chicken is cooked through and the juices run clear.

5. Divide the rice evenly among 4 bowls. Top each with one-fourth of the chicken and broccoli mixture. Drizzle with buffalo sauce and sprinkle with blue cheese.

BUDGET TRICK: The bigger the bag of rice you buy, the less you pay per serving, so if you can afford a big bag, go for it.

PER SERVING: Calories: 483; Total fat: 15g; Sodium: 2,294mg; Carbohydrates: 50g; Fiber: 3g; Sugars: 2g; Protein: 32g.

Easy Oven Cheddar Chicken Tenders

SERVES 4 | PREP TIME: 15 MINUTES | COOK TIME: 25 MINUTES

Crispy, cheesy, delightful! These chicken tenders are excellent dipped in barbecue sauce or honey mustard, if that's your speed. Boneless, skinless chicken breast cut into strips can be substituted for the tenders.

½ cup all-purpose flour

1 teaspoon salt

½ teaspoon freshly ground black pepper

1 teaspoon garlic powder

1 large egg, beaten

1 cup panko bread crumbs

1 cup shredded Cheddar cheese

1 to 1½ pounds chicken tenders

1. Preheat the oven to 400°F. Line a baking sheet with parchment paper.

2. In a shallow bowl, whisk the flour, salt, pepper, and garlic powder to combine. Place the egg in a shallow bowl or on a plate. In a third shallow bowl, stir together the panko bread crumbs and Cheddar cheese.

3. Dredge the chicken tenders in the flour mixture, then the egg, and finally in the panko and cheese mixture, coating both sides in each. Place the coated tenders on the prepared baking sheet.

4. Bake for 20 to 25 minutes, turning once about halfway through the baking time, until the chicken tenders are cooked through and beginning to brown. They will largely remain light in color, and the juices will run clear.

BUDGET TRICK: Pay attention to per-pound prices when you buy chicken. Sometimes there can be a substantial savings when you buy bulk packs and freeze the excess for later.

PER SERVING: Calories: 374; Total fat: 11g; Sodium: 866mg; Carbohydrates: 31g; Fiber: 1g; Sugars: 1g; Protein: 37g.

Spicy Cod in Tomato and Red Pepper Broth with Andouille Sausage ⑤ ⑤ ⑤

SERVES 4 | PREP TIME: 10 MINUTES | COOK TIME: 30 MINUTES

This elegant dish is perfect for special occasions. Perfectly cooked cod is served in a light, spicy broth made from tomato and red bell pepper. Andouille sausage and onion dot the dish as well. Be forewarned: This meal is for those who like a little heat.

1 tablespoon olive oil

¼ cup diced red onion

6 ounces (about 2 links) precooked andouille sausage, cubed

2 garlic cloves, minced

2 tomatoes, cut into large chunks

1 red bell pepper, cored, seeded, and cut into large chunks

1 cup water

1 pound cod, quartered

Salt

Freshly ground black pepper

1. Preheat the oven to 425°F.

2. In a large oven-safe skillet over medium heat, heat the olive oil. Add the red onion and sausage and cook for 7 to 10 minutes, stirring, until the onion begins to brown.

3. In a blender or food processor, combine the garlic, tomatoes, and red bell pepper. Process until smooth. Add the water and process to combine. Pour the tomato and red pepper mixture into the skillet and stir to combine. Bring to a boil, reduce the heat to maintain a simmer, and cook for 5 minutes. Remove from the heat.

4. Season the cod all over with salt and pepper and nestle the pieces into the sauce.

5. Bake for 10 to 15 minutes until the cod is just cooked. The layers should easily separate with a fork.

6. Place 1 piece of cod in each of 4 shallow bowls. Divide the sauce, sausage, and onion evenly among the bowls.

PER SERVING: Calories: 266; Total fat: 9g; Sodium: 575mg; Carbohydrates: 7g; Fiber: 2g; Sugars: 3g; Protein: 37g.

NUT-FREE

Crispy Coconut Drumsticks

SERVES 4 | PREP TIME: 10 MINUTES | COOK TIME: 50 MINUTES

Chicken drumsticks are such a treat for my kids, even now that they are a tween and teen. They love the hands-on style of eating them and all the ways they can be flavored and enjoyed. This version coats the drumsticks with a crispy, sweet combination of coconut and panko bread crumbs.

Nonstick cooking spray

⅓ cup shredded sweetened coconut

⅓ cup panko bread crumbs

1 teaspoon garlic powder

1 large egg

1 tablespoon 2 percent milk

1 teaspoon salt

1½ to 2 pounds chicken drumsticks

1. Preheat the oven to 425°F. Coat a 9-by-13-inch glass baking dish with nonstick cooking spray. Set aside.

2. In a shallow bowl, stir together the coconut, panko bread crumbs, and garlic powder. In another shallow bowl, whisk the egg, milk, and salt to combine.

3. Dredge the chicken in the egg mixture and then in the coconut mixture, pressing so the coating sticks. Place the coated chicken in the prepared baking dish. Spray the chicken with nonstick cooking spray.

4. Bake for 40 to 50 minutes, until the chicken is cooked through, reaching an internal temperature of 165°F, and the juices run clear.

BUDGET TRICK: Extra coconut can be stored for other recipes. Try it sprinkled on cereal, mixed into cake, or topping fruit salad.

PER SERVING: Calories: 371; Total fat: 19g; Sodium: 776mg; Carbohydrates: 11g; Fiber: 1g; Sugars: 1g; Protein: 36g.

Roasted Garlic-Paprika Chicken Breasts

SERVES 4 | PREP TIME: 10 MINUTES | COOK TIME: 45 MINUTES

Skip the boneless, skinless chicken and try bone-in, skin-on chicken breasts for a change—they have a lot more flavor. Serve this fragrant chicken with a salad or other vegetable and a carb, like mashed potatoes.

1½ to 2 pounds bone-in, skin-on chicken breasts

1 teaspoon olive oil

½ teaspoon paprika

½ teaspoon garlic powder

½ teaspoon salt

¼ teaspoon freshly ground black pepper

1. Preheat the oven to 400°F. Line a baking sheet with aluminum foil.

2. Brush the chicken all over with the olive oil.

3. In a small bowl, stir together the paprika, garlic powder, salt, and pepper. Sprinkle the spices all over the chicken. Arrange the chicken pieces on the prepared baking sheet.

4. Bake for 35 to 45 minutes, until the chicken is cooked through, reaching an internal temperature of 165°F, and the juices run clear.

5. Let cool for 10 minutes before cutting the meat from the bone.

BUDGET TRICK: **If olive oil isn't something you keep on hand, use what you have.**

PER SERVING: Calories: 305; Total fat: 17g; Sodium: 398mg; Carbohydrates: 1g; Fiber: <1g; Sugars: 0g; Protein: 36g.

30 MINUTES | DAIRY-FREE | NUT-FREE

Salmon Burgers with Avocado

SERVES 4 | PREP TIME: 15 MINUTES | COOK TIME: 10 MINUTES

Canned seafood is excellent for making patties and other seasoned dishes. In this recipe, it's used to form burger patties that are topped with avocado, onion, and more for a hearty dinner.

1 (14.75-ounce) can salmon, drained

1 large egg

½ cup bread crumbs

2 garlic cloves, minced

2 tablespoons minced fresh dill

1 teaspoon salt

½ teaspoon freshly ground black pepper

2 tablespoons canola oil

4 hamburger buns

1 avocado, peeled, halved, pitted, and sliced

4 slices red onion

1 tomato, sliced

Lettuce leaves, for serving

1. Crumble the salmon into a large bowl. If the canned salmon has skin still attached, remove it along with any large pieces of bone. Add the egg, bread crumbs, garlic, dill, salt, and pepper. Mix to combine. Form the salmon mixture into 4 patties about ¼ inch thick.

2. In a large skillet over medium heat, heat the canola oil. Add the salmon patties to the skillet and cook for about 4 minutes per side until golden.

3. Divide the buns among 4 plates. Top each with a salmon patty, avocado slices, 1 red onion slice, tomato slices, and lettuce.

BUDGET TRICK: Refrigerate leftover cut red onion in an airtight container for 7 to 10 days. It can be used in multiple recipes over multiple days.

PER SERVING: Calories: 483; Total fat: 24g; Sodium: 925mg; Carbohydrates: 39g; Fiber: 4g; Sugars: 5g; Protein: 29g.

Hoisin Beef
Skewers with
Gingery Red
Cabbage Slaw
PAGE 98

||||||||||||||||||||||||||||||||||||||||||||||||||||||||||||||||||||||||||||||||

Beef and Pork Mains

||||||||||||||||||||||||||||||||||||||||||||||||||||||||||||||||||||||

Shepherd's Pie Bowl

SERVES 4 | PREP TIME: 15 MINUTES | COOK TIME: 40 MINUTES

Here's what I like about shepherd's pie: It's comfort food, it's so bone-warming, and it's an easy one-stop shop for dinner. Here's what I don't like: It has unnecessary steps, like baking the dish once all the parts are made. This recipe solves that, trading the casserole for bowls and serving the ground beef filling over the mashed potatoes.

1 pound potatoes, peeled and diced

⅓ cup 2 percent milk

Salt

Freshly ground black pepper

2 tablespoons olive oil

3 garlic cloves, minced

1 onion, diced

2 carrots, diced

1 pound ground beef

1 large tomato, diced

1 cup frozen peas

1 teaspoon dried basil

1 teaspoon dried thyme

1. In a saucepan, combine the diced potatoes and enough water to cover by 1 inch. Bring to a boil over high heat and cook for 12 to 15 minutes, until tender. Drain and return the potatoes to the pan. Off the heat, mash the potatoes thoroughly. Add the milk, season with salt and pepper, and mash again to combine. Taste and add more salt and pepper as needed. Cover to keep warm and set aside.

2. In a large skillet over medium heat, heat the olive oil. Add the garlic, onion, and carrots. Cook for 8 to 10 minutes, stirring occasionally, until the vegetables are softened. Push to one side of the skillet and add the ground beef. Cook for about 8 minutes, stirring and breaking apart the meat, until browned and no pink remains. Drain any excess fat.

3. Stir in the tomato, peas, basil, and thyme. Season with salt and pepper. Cook for 4 to 5 minutes, stirring, until the tomato is softened.

4. Divide the mashed potatoes evenly among 4 bowls. Top each with one-fourth of the ground beef mixture.

PER SERVING: Calories: 405; Total fat: 18g; Sodium: 167mg; Carbohydrates: 33g; Fiber: 6g; Sugars: 8g; Protein: 29g.

Marinated Eye Round Steaks

**SERVES 4 | PREP TIME: 5 MINUTES, PLUS 30 MINUTES TO MARINATE |
COOK TIME: 10 MINUTES**

Inexpensive cuts of beef like eye round steaks can be tough. But with the right treatment—like marinating in an acidic marinade as we do here—they can be a delightful budget-friendly change from the usual. The flavor of these steaks is rich thanks to the tangy red wine vinegar and familiar flavors of garlic and onion. Serve these with mashed potatoes and your favorite veggie side dish.

¼ cup red wine vinegar

1 teaspoon salt

1 teaspoon
    garlic powder

1 teaspoon
    onion powder

¼ teaspoon freshly
    ground black pepper

4 (5-ounce) eye
    round steaks

1. In a small bowl, whisk the vinegar, salt, garlic powder, onion powder, and pepper to blend. Place the steaks in a resealable container or bag and pour the marinade over them. Seal the container and refrigerate for 30 minutes, turning the steaks once.

2. Heat a skillet over medium heat. Add the steaks, discarding any excess marinade. Cook for 3 to 5 minutes per side, flipping once, or until your desired doneness.

BUDGET TRICK: Looking for more ideas for serving these? Transform the most inexpensive lettuce into a steakhouse-inspired salad by topping it with these steaks, thinly sliced against the grain, along with cheese, croutons, and your favorite dressing.

PER SERVING: Calories: 243; Total fat: 13g; Sodium: 651mg; Carbohydrates: 1g; Fiber: <1g; Sugars: 0g; Protein: 29g.

Bacon, Egg, and Cheese Burger Salads

SERVES 4 | PREP TIME: 15 MINUTES | COOK TIME: 35 MINUTES

Have you ever had a breakfast burger? It's a juicy burger topped with a fried egg and other toppings—and it's a great way to start the day. This salad is inspired by that glorious creation, but instead of a bun, all the salty, meaty, melty goodness is served on a dressing-free salad. That runny yolk provides all the creaminess this salad needs to come together.

1 pound ground beef

Salt

Freshly ground black pepper

4 slices Cheddar cheese

4 bacon slices, chopped

1 head iceberg lettuce, chopped

2 tomatoes, chopped

4 large eggs

1. Season the ground beef all over with salt and pepper. Divide it into 4 even pieces and press each piece into a patty about ¼ inch thick. Press your thumb into the center of each patty to reduce shrinkage during cooking.

2. Heat a large skillet over medium heat. Add the burgers to the skillet and cook for 6 to 8 minutes per side, flipping once, or until your desired doneness. Do not press down on the burgers while cooking—this pushes out all the juicy juices. When the burgers are nearly cooked (about 1 minute left), topped each with 1 slice of Cheddar cheese.

3. While the burgers cook, heat a small skillet over medium heat. Add the bacon and cook for 5 to 7 minutes, until browned. Transfer the bacon pieces to a paper towel–lined plate to drain, leaving the fat in the pan. Set aside.

4. Divide the lettuce and tomatoes evenly among 4 plates. Top each with a burger and one-fourth of the bacon.

5. Place the small skillet with the reserved bacon fat over medium heat. Crack 1 egg into the skillet and cook for 4 to 5 minutes, flipping once about halfway through the cooking time, until the white is set. Top a salad with the egg. Repeat with the remaining eggs.

6. Season the salads with a slight sprinkle of salt and pepper.

BUDGET TRICK: **If your family is like mine, you like bacon in dishes but seldom can use a full pound in a week. Good news: There's a way to extend the life of your bacon. When you bring it home, remove what you need, and then freeze the rest in an airtight container or freezer-safe bag for 4 to 6 months. Cut off just what you need whenever you need it and cook from frozen. Just add a couple more minutes to the cook time.**

PER SERVING: Calories: 417; Total fat: 25g; Sodium: 452mg; Carbohydrates: 7g; Fiber: 2g; Sugars: 5g; Protein: 40g.

Hoisin Beef Skewers with Gingery Red Cabbage Slaw

SERVES 4 | PREP TIME: 15 MINUTES | COOK TIME: 15 MINUTES

Glazed with a rich, slightly sweet sauce, these beef skewers are delightful with the cool, tangy slaw. And it takes just a few minutes for the flavors of the slaw to come together and shine.

FOR THE SKEWERS

1 pound sirloin steak, cut into 1-inch pieces

3 tablespoons hoisin sauce

1 tablespoon seasoned rice vinegar

1 garlic clove, minced

FOR THE SLAW

4 cups thinly shredded red cabbage

¼ cup seasoned rice vinegar

2 tablespoons soy sauce

1 tablespoon grated peeled fresh ginger

1 teaspoon garlic powder

TO MAKE THE SKEWERS

1. Preheat the broiler. Line a baking sheet with aluminum foil.

2. Thread the steak onto 4 skewers, dividing it evenly among them. Place the skewers on the prepared baking sheet.

3. In a small bowl, whisk the hoisin sauce, vinegar, and garlic to combine. Brush the skewers with the sauce.

4. Broil for 13 to 15 minutes, flipping once about halfway through the cooking time and brushing them with more sauce. When done, remove the skewers from the oven and brush with the remaining sauce.

TO MAKE THE SLAW

5. While the skewers cook, in a large bowl, combine the cabbage, vinegar, soy sauce, ginger, and garlic powder. Toss well to combine. Let sit for 10 minutes and toss again.

6. Evenly divide the slaw among 4 plates. Top each with a hoisin beef skewer.

PER SERVING: Calories: 310; Total fat: 15g; Sodium: 964mg; Carbohydrates: 18g; Fiber: 2g; Sugars: 12g; Protein: 25g.

One-Pot Red Beans and Rice

SERVES 4 | PREP TIME: 10 MINUTES | COOK TIME: 35 MINUTES

My daughter avoids spicy foods. My son wants to like them but has a low tolerance. And I love them. So recipes like this are perfect for us because everyone can adjust the flavor to their desired spice level. Also, the andouille sausage mellows with cooking, so don't worry about it being too spicy.

1 tablespoon olive oil

2 links precooked andouille sausage, cut into ¼-inch pieces

1 small onion, diced

1 small red bell pepper, diced

1 celery stalk, diced

2 teaspoons garlic powder

2 teaspoons paprika

2 (15.5-ounce) cans red kidney beans, drained and rinsed

1½ cups Slow Cooker Chicken Stock (page 136) or store-bought chicken broth

1 cup raw white rice

Hot sauce, for serving

1. In a large sauté pan or skillet with a lid over medium heat, heat the olive oil. Add the sausage, onion, red bell pepper, and celery. Cook for 10 to 12 minutes, stirring frequently, until the vegetables are softened and the sausage is warmed.

2. Stir in the garlic powder, paprika, kidney beans, chicken stock, and rice. Reduce the heat to medium-low. Cover the pan and cook for 15 to 20 minutes, until the liquid is absorbed.

3. Season with hot sauce as desired.

BUDGET TRICK: Precooked sausages often come in packages of 6. Divide them into portions of 2 each, wrap, and freeze for 1 to 2 months. Then just grab a couple from the freezer for dishes like this and thaw as needed.

PER SERVING: Calories: 514; Total fat: 9g; Sodium: 739mg; Carbohydrates: 82g; Fiber: 17g; Sugars: 7g; Protein: 29g.

Bacon-Cheeseburger Meatloaf

SERVES 4 | PREP TIME: 15 MINUTES | COOK TIME: 40 MINUTES

Meatloaf was a staple of my childhood kitchen, though I was never a fan of the ketchup-coated, crunchy onion–filled dish. Fortunately, my kids have encouraged me to give meatloaf another try. I'm glad I listened because I learned that versions like this salty bacon–studded, cheese-filled, barbecue-topped meatloaf are super delicious and satisfying.

Nonstick cooking spray

1 pound ground beef

4 bacon slices, cooked, cooled, and crumbled

1 large egg

1 cup shredded Cheddar cheese

1 cup bread crumbs

⅓ cup 2 percent milk

1 tablespoon Worcestershire sauce

1 teaspoon salt

1 teaspoon garlic powder

¼ teaspoon freshly ground black pepper

¼ cup barbecue sauce

1. Preheat the oven to 375°F. Coat a standard loaf pan with nonstick cooking spray.

2. In a large bowl, stir together the ground beef, crumbled bacon, egg, Cheddar cheese, bread crumbs, milk, Worcestershire sauce, salt, garlic powder, and pepper. Use your clean hands, if necessary, to get the ingredients fully combined. Press the meat mixture into the prepared loaf pan, creating a single, flat layer. Top with the barbecue sauce, spreading it end to end.

3. Bake for 40 minutes, or until the meatloaf reaches an internal temperature of 160°F.

4. Let cool for 10 minutes. Loosen the edges with a butter knife. Cut the meatloaf into slices and gently remove from the pan to serve.

BUDGET TRICK: **Although this recipe is made with beef, other ground meats can be substituted. Ground turkey is especially good and often less expensive.**

PER SERVING: Calories: 474; Total fat: 24g; Sodium: 1,239mg; Carbohydrates: 24g; Fiber: 1g; Sugars: 8g; Protein: 38g.

5 INGREDIENTS | DAIRY-FREE | GLUTEN-FREE | NUT-FREE | ONE POT

Pork Tenderloin with Roasted Red Onion and Grapes

SERVES 4 | PREP TIME: 10 MINUTES | COOK TIME: 40 MINUTES

Sweet and savory flavors go hand in hand in dishes like this bold pork tenderloin. If you haven't had roasted grapes, it's time you did. They retain all the pleasant sweetness while becoming richer in flavor.

1½ pounds pork
   tenderloin

Salt

Freshly ground
   black pepper

1 red onion, cut
   into 8 pieces

1 cup seedless
   red grapes

1 tablespoon canola oil

1. Preheat the oven to 425°F.

2. Season the pork all over with salt and pepper and place it in a 9-by-13-inch glass baking dish. Surround the pork with the red onion and grapes, drizzle with canola oil, and season the red onion and grapes with salt and pepper.

3. Bake for 30 minutes.

4. Using a basting brush, baste the pork with the pan juices. Bake for 5 to 10 minutes more, or until the pork reaches an internal temperature of 140°F.

5. Let the pork rest for 5 minutes before thinly slicing and serving topped with the red onion and grapes.

BUDGET TRICK: **Grocery stores put out pre-packed bags of grapes, but you don't have to buy them that way. Instead, use a different bag to select only as many as you need.**

PER SERVING: Calories: 237; Total fat: 7g; Sodium: 106mg; Carbohydrates: 8g; Fiber: 1g; Sugars: 5g; Protein: 37g.

One-Pan Pork Chops with Apples, Red Onion, and Red Cabbage

SERVES 4 | PREP TIME: 15 MINUTES | COOK TIME: 20 MINUTES

Browned bone-in pork chops that have been rubbed all over with a variety of herbaceous seasonings have an almost smoky flavor when cooked. The flavor is a lovely foil to the bright, tangy, sweet slaw that accompanies these chops.

2 tablespoons olive oil

½ teaspoon salt, plus more for seasoning

½ teaspoon garlic powder

½ teaspoon dried rosemary

⅛ teaspoon freshly ground black pepper, plus more for seasoning

1 pound bone-in thin-cut pork chops

4 cups shredded red cabbage

1 small red onion, cut into 8 pieces

1 Granny Smith apple, peeled and diced

1. In a large skillet over medium heat, heat the olive oil.

2. In a small bowl, stir together the salt, garlic powder, rosemary, and pepper. Season the pork chops all over with the spice mix. Add the seasoned chops to the skillet in a single layer and cook for about 4 minutes, or until browned. Flip the chops and cook for 3 to 4 minutes more, or until the chops are lightly browned on each side and reach an internal temperature of 145°F. Transfer the pork chops to a plate and tent loosely with aluminum foil to keep warm.

3. Add the cabbage, red onion, and apple to the skillet. Season lightly with salt and pepper. Cook for 8 to 10 minutes, stirring, until crisp-tender. Evenly divide the chops and cabbage among 4 plates.

PER SERVING: Calories: 252; Total fat: 14g; Sodium: 717mg; Carbohydrates: 14g; Fiber: 3g; Sugars: 9g; Protein: 18g.

Boneless Pork Chops with Creamy Roasted Red Pepper, Spinach, and Garlic Sauce

SERVES 4 | PREP TIME: 10 MINUTES | COOK TIME: 35 MINUTES

Pork chops are good, but pork chops served in a flavorful, creamy sauce are excellent. This sauce builds flavor as it cooks, the bit of flour thickening it slightly. But more than that, this dish feels fancy and beautiful—even though it's actually pretty easy to make.

2 tablespoons canola oil

2 teaspoons all-purpose flour

Salt

Freshly ground black pepper

4 (5-ounce) boneless pork chops

2 large shallots, thinly sliced (about 1 cup)

½ cup chopped roasted red pepper

1 cup frozen chopped spinach

3 garlic cloves, minced

1 cup Slow Cooker Chicken Stock (page 136) or store-bought chicken broth

½ cup half-and-half

1. In a large skillet over medium heat, heat the canola oil.

2. Place the flour in a small bowl, season it with salt and pepper, and stir to combine. Season the pork chops all over with the seasoned flour and add them to the skillet in a single layer. Cook for 3 to 4 minutes per side, until browned. Remove the pork chops from the skillet.

3. Add the shallots to the skillet and cook for 3 to 5 minutes, until softened. Stir in the roasted red pepper, spinach, and garlic. Cover the skillet and cook for 3 minutes. Uncover and whisk in the chicken stock.

4. Return the pork to the skillet and mix well, covering it with the sauce. Re-cover the skillet and reduce the heat to medium-low. Simmer for 8 to 10 minutes, until the sauce is slightly thickened.

CONTINUED

5. Stir in the half-and-half. Cook for just
about 2 minutes, stirring, to allow it to integrate
with the sauce. Don't overcook it or the sauce
will break. Serve the pork chops covered with the
creamy sauce.

BUDGET TRICK: **If you aren't normally a half-and-
half user, buy the smallest container possible and
plan to use some for other dishes like Cheesy Sausage Dip (page 119).**

PER SERVING: Calories: 329; Total fat: 17g;
Sodium: 386mg; Carbohydrates: 13g; Fiber: 2g; Sugars: 5g;
Protein: 34g.

Slow Cooker Cilantro-Lime Pork Carnitas Tacos

SERVES 4 | PREP TIME: 15 MINUTES | COOK TIME: 10 HOURS

Don't you just love a recipe that you can toss together in the morning and have ready and waiting when you return in the evening? That's this recipe. Slow-cooked and full of flavor, these carnitas are a wonderful filling for corn tortillas. Heat the tortillas just before serving for best results.

1 (1½- to 2-pound) pork butt or pork roast

Salt

Freshly ground black pepper

1 teaspoon dried oregano

1 teaspoon ground cumin

1 onion, diced

2 garlic cloves, crushed

1 tablespoon olive oil

Juice of 1 lime

2 tablespoons chopped fresh cilantro

12 to 16 (6-inch) corn tortillas

1. Season the pork all over with salt, pepper, the oregano, and the cumin. Place the pork in a slow cooker. Arrange the onion and garlic around the pork and drizzle with the olive oil. Sprinkle with additional salt and pepper.

2. Cover the cooker and cook on low heat for about 10 hours. Using two forks, shred the pork in the cooker.

3. Drizzle the pork with the lime juice and sprinkle with the cilantro. Toss well to combine. Serve in tortillas with desired taco toppings.

4. Refrigerate any leftovers in an airtight container for 4 to 5 days.

COOKING TIP: No slow cooker? Preheat the oven to 325°F. Season the pork as directed in step 1 and place it into a Dutch oven. Surround the pork with the onion and garlic and drizzle with olive oil. Cover the pot and bake for 3 to 3½ hours, or until the pork can be pulled apart easily using two forks. Finish the recipe as instructed in steps 3 and 4.

PER SERVING: Calories: 758; Total fat: 47g; Sodium: 157mg; Carbohydrates: 38g; Fiber: 6g; Sugars: 2g; Protein: 45g.

Teriyaki Pineapple and Pork Kebabs

SERVES 4 | PREP TIME: 15 MINUTES | COOK TIME: 25 MINUTES

One of the things I love about kebabs is how you can pack so many different flavors onto the skewers. In this case, meaty pork, sweet pineapple, and zesty red onion are bathed in a light coating of teriyaki for a decadent flavor bomb on a stick. So good.

1 pound boneless pork chops, each cut into 8 pieces

1 (8-ounce) can pineapple chunks, drained

1 small red onion, cut into 8 pieces

2 tablespoons teriyaki sauce

Salt

Freshly ground black pepper

1. Preheat the oven to 375°F. Line a baking sheet with parchment paper.

2. Thread the pork, pineapple, and red onion onto 8 skewers, alternating between pork, pineapple, and red onion until all the ingredients are used. Place the skewers on the prepared baking sheet. Brush each with teriyaki sauce and lightly season with salt and pepper.

3. Bake for 10 minutes. Flip the skewers and baste with more teriyaki sauce. Bake for 8 to 10 minutes more. Turn the skewers. If they aren't yet cooked through (the meat will be firm to the touch), baste with additional teriyaki sauce and return to the oven for 5 minutes more.

BUDGET TRICK: You don't need to buy that little can of pineapple to make this. If you want to buy a more cost-effective larger can, simply portion out 16 pineapple chunks (2 per skewer) to substitute. Refrigerate leftovers in an airtight container for up to 5 days and consider making Sheet Pan Teriyaki Beef Subs with Red Peppers and Pineapple (page 49) with the leftovers.

PER SERVING: Calories: 185; Total fat: 5g; Sodium: 516mg; Carbohydrates: 13g; Fiber: 1g; Sugars: 11g; Protein: 24g.

Sesame Beef Rice Bowls

SERVES 4 | PREP TIME: 10 MINUTES, PLUS 30 MINUTES TO MARINATE | COOK TIME: 25 MINUTES

Rice bowls are one of my all-time favorite dinners because you get to layer and mix up flavors—including savory and sweet! Plus, served over warm rice, they are downright comfort food. These rice bowls feature a sweet-salty marinated steak, red bell pepper, and lots of rice and sesame seeds.

¼ **cup soy sauce**

¼ **cup packed light brown sugar**

2 garlic cloves, minced

1½ **pounds flank steak**

1 tablespoon olive oil

1 red bell pepper, thinly sliced

1 bunch scallions, white and light green parts cut into 1-inch pieces, dark green parts thinly sliced and reserved

2 cups cooked rice

Sesame seeds, for garnish

1. In a small bowl, whisk the soy sauce, brown sugar, and garlic to blend. Place the flank steak in a resealable container or bag and pour in half the sauce. Seal the container and refrigerate to marinate for at least 30 minutes. Reserve the remaining sauce.

2. Preheat the boiler. Line a baking sheet with aluminum foil.

3. Remove the flank steak from the marinade and place it on the prepared baking sheet.

4. Broil for 4 to 6 minutes per side. Let rest for 10 minutes before thinly slicing across the grain.

5. While the steak rests, in a large skillet over medium heat, heat the olive oil. Add the red bell pepper and white and light green scallion parts. Cook, stirring, for 8 to 10 minutes until the vegetables are softened. Add the reserved sauce and cook for 2 to 3 minutes more. Add the flank steak and toss to coat. Remove from the heat.

6. Divide the rice evenly among 4 bowls. Top each with one-fourth of the steak mixture. Sprinkle with sesame seeds and the scallion dark greens.

PER SERVING: Calories: 477; Total fat: 14g; Sodium: 1,000mg; Carbohydrates: 44g; Fiber: 1g; Sugars: 13g; Protein: 42g.

Country-Fried Steak and Onions

SERVES 4 | PREP TIME: 15 MINUTES | COOK TIME: 30 MINUTES

When I was a little girl, my grandmother and I would often have early dinners in restaurants with an early-bird menu. I could order anything, she told me. So I would mix it up between dishes I knew I liked and ones that sounded interesting. Among those? Chicken-fried steak (sometimes called country-fried steak). I developed a taste for the meaty, breaded steak. This at-home version reminds me of childhood with a twist, thanks to the fried onions.

2 tablespoons olive oil, divided

2 onions, quartered and sliced

Salt

Freshly ground black pepper

4 cube steaks

2 tablespoons all-purpose flour

½ teaspoon paprika

½ teaspoon garlic powder

1 large egg, beaten

⅓ cup bread crumbs

1. In a large skillet over medium heat, heat 1 tablespoon of olive oil. Add the onions and season lightly with salt and pepper. Cook for 10 to 12 minutes, stirring, until golden brown. Remove the onions from the skillet. Set the skillet aside.

2. Season the steaks all over with salt and pepper. In a shallow bowl, stir together the flour, paprika, garlic powder, ½ teaspoon of salt, and ¼ teaspoon of pepper. In a second bowl, whisk the egg until smooth. Place the bread crumbs in a third shallow bowl.

3. Dredge the seasoned steaks in the flour mixture, thoroughly coating them, then in the egg, and finally in the bread crumbs, coating both sides.

4. Return the skillet to medium heat and heat the remaining 1 tablespoon of olive oil. Working in batches as needed, add the steaks, adding more oil between batches to prevent sticking. Cook the steaks for about 5 minutes per side until browned and cooked through. Serve topped with the onions.

PER SERVING: Calories: 328; Total fat: 17g; Sodium: 392mg; Carbohydrates: 14g; Fiber: 2g; Sugars: 3g; Protein: 27g.

Rich Pork Stir-Fry with Hoisin Garlic-Ginger Sauce

SERVES 4 | PREP TIME: 10 MINUTES | COOK TIME: 20 MINUTES

My kids say this pork dish reminds them of a Korean dish I have made before. Its rich garlicky, gingery flavor is excellent for topping rice, piling onto a salad, or in a lettuce wrap.

1 pound ground pork

4 garlic cloves, minced

1 tablespoon grated peeled fresh ginger

4 scallions, sliced, dark green parts reserved

2 tablespoons hoisin sauce

1 tablespoon soy sauce

1 teaspoon light brown sugar

1. In a large skillet over medium heat, brown the ground pork for 6 to 8 minutes, stirring occasionally with a spatula to break up the meat, until no pink remains.

2. Add the garlic, ginger, and white and light green scallion parts to the skillet. Cook for 2 to 3 minutes, stirring, until the vegetables begin to soften.

3. Stir in the hoisin sauce, soy sauce, and brown sugar to combine. Cook for 3 to 4 minutes, stirring occasionally, until fully coated. The sauce should reduce while cooking. Remove from the heat.

4. Sprinkle with the dark green scallion parts.

BUDGET TRICK: **It's okay to substitute other ground meats if they are on sale. Turkey or beef might be a more budget-friendly option.**

PER SERVING: Calories: 332; Total fat: 24g; Sodium: 421mg; Carbohydrates: 7g; Fiber: 1g; Sugars: 4g; Protein: 20g.

Tomato
Ricotta Toast
with Basil,
PAGE 114

‖‖‖

CHAPTER EIGHT

Sides and Snacks

‖‖‖

Roasted Cauliflower with Gorgonzola and Pomegranate

SERVES 4 | PREP TIME: 10 MINUTES | COOK TIME: 40 MINUTES

Tender roasted cauliflower with caramelization on the outside is such a treat by itself. But when you mix it with bold Gorgonzola cheese, earthy parsley, and bright pomegranate arils, it's a delight. This dish is also excellent as leftovers. Take some for lunch!

1 head cauliflower, leaves removed, broken into small florets, stem diced

2 tablespoons olive oil

Salt

Freshly ground black pepper

¼ cup Gorgonzola cheese

2 tablespoons chopped fresh parsley

2 tablespoons pomegranate arils

1. Preheat the oven to 400°F. Line a baking sheet with parchment paper.

2. Spread the cauliflower on the prepared baking sheet. Drizzle with the olive oil and season with salt and pepper.

3. Bake for 25 minutes. Stir. Bake for 10 to 15 minutes more, until browned in spots and tender. Transfer the hot cauliflower to a serving bowl.

4. Add the Gorgonzola cheese and toss to combine. Top with the parsley and pomegranate arils to serve.

BUDGET TRICK: Whole pomegranates are usually cheaper than the plucked arils, but removing the arils from the pomegranate can be messy. I cut through the skin so I can break the pomegranate into 4 pieces and then remove the arils with my fingers, brushing them into a bowl. Check out online tutorials for good visual descriptions.

PER SERVING: Calories: 126; Total fat: 9g; Sodium: 114mg; Carbohydrates: 9g; Fiber: 4g; Sugars: 4g; Protein: 5g.

Peas with Mint, Shallots, and Orange Zest

SERVES 4 | PREP TIME: 10 MINUTES | COOK TIME: 15 MINUTES

Sweet peas dance with cooling aromatic mint, sunny orange, and sweet shallot in this quick and easy side dish. It's a step outside the ordinary, which makes this an excellent option for potlucks, too.

2 cups frozen peas

1 tablespoon olive oil

1 shallot, chopped (about ½ cup)

1 tablespoon grated orange zest

1 teaspoon finely chopped fresh mint

Salt

Freshly ground black pepper

1. Bring a medium pot of water to a boil over high heat. Add the peas and cook according to the package directions. Drain and transfer to a large bowl.

2. In a small skillet over medium heat, heat the olive oil. Add the shallot and cook for 5 to 7 minutes, stirring occasionally, until lightly browned and softened. Add the shallot and olive oil to the peas along with the orange zest and mint. Stir well. Taste and season with salt and pepper as needed.

BUDGET TRICK: Of all the herbs, mint is one of the easiest to grow, and it will come back year after year. Try growing some in your yard or a pot and saving it for later, too. Mint can be whirled with a little water in a blender and frozen in ice cube trays for later use.

PER SERVING: Calories: 101; Total fat: 4g; Sodium: 83mg; Carbohydrates: 14g; Fiber: 3g; Sugars: 5g; Protein: 4g.

Tomato Ricotta Toast with Basil

SERVES 4 | PREP TIME: 10 MINUTES | COOK TIME: 10 MINUTES

Forget avocado toast. You want to try this flavorful, easy spin on bruschetta. Normally bland ricotta gets a big boost of flavor with bright basil. And the tomatoes, cooked just until they burst, add a juicy tang to the dish.

4 slices white bread

¼ cup ricotta

1 tablespoon finely chopped fresh basil

½ teaspoon salt

¼ teaspoon freshly ground black pepper

Pinch red pepper flakes

1 teaspoon olive oil

1 cup cherry tomatoes

1. Toast the bread. While it's toasting, in a small bowl, stir together the ricotta, basil, salt, pepper, and red pepper flakes. Set aside.

2. In a large skillet over medium heat, heat the olive oil. Add the tomatoes and cook for 8 to 10 minutes, shaking the pan occasionally, until the tomatoes burst.

3. Spread the ricotta mixture on the toast, evenly dividing it among the slices.

4. Using a fork, crush the tomatoes. Spoon the tomato mixture over the ricotta, evenly dividing it among the toasts.

BUDGET TRICK: **The best bread for a dish like this is the loaf you have. Rye, sourdough, wheat, or Italian provides good results.**

PER SERVING: Calories: 126; Total fat: 4g; Sodium: 482mg; Carbohydrates: 17g; Fiber: 1g; Sugars: 2g; Protein: 5g.

Garlic-Sesame Green Beans

SERVES 4 | PREP TIME: 10 MINUTES | COOK TIME: 15 MINUTES

What makes boring green beans stand out as a side dish? Giving them a flavorful boost with a scintillating sauce like the garlicky one featured here.

1 pound green
  beans, trimmed

1 tablespoon olive oil

3 garlic cloves, minced

1 tablespoon soy sauce

Salt

Freshly ground
  black pepper

1 teaspoon
  sesame seeds

1. In a saucepan, steam or boil the green beans for 8 to 10 minutes until crisp-tender. Drain and return to the pan. Set aside.

2. In a small skillet over medium heat, heat the olive oil. Add the garlic and cook for 1 to 2 minutes, or until fragrant. Remove from the heat and stir in the soy sauce. Pour the sauce over the green beans and stir well to combine. Season with salt and pepper as desired, and sprinkle with sesame seeds. Serve hot.

BUDGET TRICK: **Frozen or fresh green beans will work in this dish. Use whatever is less expensive. Or grow and freeze your own. Green beans can be frozen whole without blanching for 4 to 6 months.**

PER SERVING: Calories: 75; Total fat: 4g; Sodium: 233mg; Carbohydrates: 9g; Fiber: 4g; Sugars: 4g; Protein: 3g.

Broccoli with Lemon-Garlic Sauce

SERVES 4 | PREP TIME: 10 MINUTES | COOK TIME: 10 MINUTES

Broccoli is probably the most-consumed vegetable in my house. That's why we look for so many ways to enjoy it—like this tangy, garlicky version that's ready in minutes.

4 cups broccoli florets

1 tablespoon olive oil

2 garlic cloves, minced

1 tablespoon freshly squeezed lemon juice

Salt

Freshly ground black pepper

1. In a saucepan, steam or boil the broccoli for 6 to 8 minutes until just fork-tender (you don't want it too soft). Drain and return to the saucepan. Set aside

2. In a small skillet over medium heat, heat the olive oil. Add the garlic and cook for 1 to 2 minutes, stirring, until fragrant. Remove from the heat and stir in the lemon juice. Pour the sauce over the broccoli. Season with salt and pepper.

BUDGET TRICK: **If frozen broccoli is on sale, use it in place of fresh broccoli here. It will make this dish even faster to prepare.**

PER SERVING: Calories: 63; Total fat: 4g; Sodium: 21mg; Carbohydrates: 5g; Fiber: 2g; Sugars: 2g; Protein: 1g.

Sautéed Asparagus with Shallots and Parmesan

SERVES 4 | PREP TIME: 10 MINUTES | COOK TIME: 10 MINUTES

When crocuses begin emerging and daffodils make their sunny appearance, it's time for asparagus, too. Without a doubt, spring is the best time to make this simple but flavorful dish, when asparagus is at its freshest, least expensive, and most plentiful.

2 tablespoons olive oil

1 pound asparagus, woody ends trimmed, cut into 1-inch pieces

1 shallot, quartered and thinly sliced

Salt

Freshly ground black pepper

¼ cup freshly grated Parmesan cheese

1. In a large skillet over medium heat, heat the olive oil. Add the asparagus and shallot. Season with salt and pepper. Cook for 8 to 10 minutes, stirring occasionally, until the vegetables are softened and beginning to brown. The asparagus should be crisp-tender.

2. Sprinkle with the Parmesan cheese and stir vigorously to coat. Remove from the heat and serve immediately.

BUDGET TRICK: **Fresh Parmesan can be pricey. If it's outside your budget, try powdered Parmesan or omit it. It's a slightly different dish—but every bit as mouthwatering.**

PER SERVING: Calories: 129; Total fat: 9g; Sodium: 121mg; Carbohydrates: 9g; Fiber: 2g; Sugars: 4g; Protein: 6g.

White Bean Artichoke Dip

SERVES 4 | PREP TIME: 15 MINUTES

Chickpeas are the most popular ingredient for hummus-like dips, but I love the flavor and texture of cannellini beans even more. They render the dip smooth and creamy and pair well with so many flavors. This one is robust with cheese, garlic, and meaty artichoke hearts. Serve it with crackers, veggies, crostini, and more.

1 (15.5-ounce) can cannellini beans, drained and rinsed

1 garlic clove, crushed

2 tablespoons grated Parmesan cheese

Salt

Freshly ground black pepper

2 tablespoons olive oil

½ cup chopped artichoke hearts (frozen and defrosted or canned)

½ teaspoon dried oregano

1. In a food processor, combine the cannellini beans, garlic, and Parmesan cheese. Season with salt and pepper. Pulse until chopped.

2. Add the olive oil and process until smooth. Transfer the white bean mixture to a bowl. Stir in the artichoke hearts and oregano.

PER SERVING: Calories: 174; Total fat: 9g; Sodium: 162mg; Carbohydrates: 18g; Fiber: 7g; Sugars: 0g; Protein: 8g.

Cheesy Sausage Dip

SERVES 4 | PREP TIME: 10 MINUTES | COOK TIME: 25 MINUTES

Creamy, melty, and satisfying, this cheese dip is studded with sausage. It's a wonderful treat, perfect for serving at gatherings with dippers like veggies (try broccoli!), crackers, or bread.

3 sweet or hot Italian sausages

½ cup water

1 tablespoon unsalted butter

1 tablespoon all-purpose flour

1 cup half-and-half

1 scallion, thinly sliced, whites, light greens, and dark greens separated

1 teaspoon dry mustard

4 ounces Cheddar cheese, grated (about 1 cup)

¼ cup diced tomato

1. In a large skillet over medium heat, combine the sausage and water. Cover the skillet and bring to a boil. Cook for 10 minutes. Remove the cover and cook for 5 to 7 minutes more, turning, until the sausages are browned on all sides. Transfer to paper towels to drain. Let cool and then dice.

2. In a large saucepan over medium heat, melt the butter. Whisk in the flour until fully combined.

3. A little at a time and while whisking constantly, add the half-and-half until it's all incorporated. Stir in the scallion whites and light green parts and the dry mustard. Cook, stirring, for 3 to 4 minutes until the mixture is very hot. It should be vigorously steaming but not yet boiling.

4. A little at a time and stirring constantly, add the Cheddar cheese until fully combined.

5. Stir in the diced sausage. Cook for 3 to 4 minutes more, stirring occasionally, until the sausage is hot. Pour the cheese dip into a serving bowl. Top with the tomato and dark green parts scallion parts.

PER SERVING: Calories: 385; Total fat: 33g; Sodium: 570mg; Carbohydrates: 7g; Fiber: <1g; Sugars: 3g; Protein: 18g.

Rustic Blueberry-Apple Pie,
PAGE 124

CHAPTER NINE

||||||||||||||||||||||||||||||||

Desserts

||||||||||||||||||||||||||||||||||||

30 MINUTES | NUT-FREE | ONE POT | VEGETARIAN

Hot Cocoa Mug Cake

SERVES 1 | PREP TIME: 5 MINUTES | COOK TIME: 1 MINUTE 30 SECONDS

Mug cakes are the greatest thing to happen to dessert . . . maybe ever. And my kids are crazy for them. It's an easy way to enjoy a sweet treat without having to make a whole big batch of something. And it's ready in minutes. This one has the flavor of hot cocoa in cake form.

1 single-serve packet hot cocoa mix

2 tablespoons all-purpose flour

¼ teaspoon baking powder

¼ cup 2 percent milk

1 teaspoon canola oil

1 tablespoon chocolate chips

Powdered sugar, for dusting

1. In a mug, stir together the hot cocoa mix, flour, and baking powder. Add the milk and canola oil and stir well to combine, being careful to get the spoon into the corners where the dry mixture likes to hide. Stir in the chocolate chips.

2. Microwave on high power for 90 seconds. The cake will rise and be springy to the touch. Dust with powdered sugar, let cool slightly, and dig in.

BUDGET TRICK: Chocolate chips are least expensive in December. Stock up for the whole year then.

PER SERVING: Calories: 275; Total fat: 13g; Sodium: 338mg; Carbohydrates: 39g; Fiber: 2g; Sugars: 23g; Protein: 6g.

5 INGREDIENTS | 30 MINUTES | GLUTEN-FREE | NO-COOK | NUT-FREE | VEGETARIAN

Raspberry Milkshake

SERVES 1 | PREP TIME: 5 MINUTES

A good milkshake is a creamy, fruity joy! This one has the bright flavors of raspberries throughout. Consider this a blueprint for further creativity: Use other frozen fruit in place of the raspberries, as desired.

1 cup vanilla ice cream

½ cup 2 percent milk

½ cup frozen raspberries

Whipped cream, for garnish

In a blender, combine the ice cream, milk, and raspberries. Pulse until smooth, about 1 minute. Transfer to a glass and top with whipped cream.

BUDGET TRICK: **If you grow your own berries, don't forget to freeze some for later to enjoy the "fruits" of your labor any time.**

PER SERVING: Calories: 378; Total fat: 17g; Sodium: 179mg; Carbohydrates: 46g; Fiber: 6g; Sugars: 37g; Protein: 10g.

Rustic Blueberry-Apple Pie

SERVES 6 | PREP TIME: 10 MINUTES | COOK TIME: 35 MINUTES

Rustic pies, sometimes called galettes, are an easy way to enjoy pie without the extra prep of properly forming a piecrust. This one is filled with blueberries and apples—a scrumptious fruit combination. Serve it with a scoop of vanilla ice cream, if you like.

1 refrigerated piecrust, at room temperature

1 cup frozen blueberries

1 Granny Smith apple, diced

2 tablespoons sugar

1 tablespoon cornstarch

1. Preheat the oven to 400°F. Line a baking sheet with parchment paper.

2. Unroll the piecrust onto the prepared baking sheet.

3. In a large bowl, stir together the blueberries, apple, sugar, and cornstarch. Spread the fruit mixture in the center of the crust. Fold the edges of the crust up and around the filling.

4. Bake for 30 to 35 minutes, until the fruit is cooked and the crust is golden brown.

BUDGET TRICK: **No plans to use the second piecrust? Freeze it for later. It will keep for 4 to 6 months until the next pie craving hits.**

PER SERVING: Calories: 183; Total fat: 8g; Sodium: 174mg; Carbohydrates: 29g; Fiber: 1g; Sugars: 10g; Protein: <1g.

Pear-Berry Hand Pies

SERVES 4 | PREP TIME: 15 MINUTES | COOK TIME: 30 MINUTES

With a flaky piecrust exterior and a sweet, fruity interior, these hand pies are a decadent way to end a meal. Serve them with a scoop of cool, creamy vanilla ice cream for an extra-special treat.

1 large pear, cut into ½-inch dice

½ cup diced berries of choice

1 tablespoon light brown sugar

1 teaspoon all-purpose flour

¼ teaspoon salt

1 refrigerated piecrust, at room temperature, quartered

1 teaspoon canola oil

Coarse sugar, for dusting

1. Preheat the oven to 350°F. Line a baking sheet with parchment paper.

2. In a large bowl, stir together the pear, berries, brown sugar, flour, and salt. Divide the pear mixture evenly among the 4 pieces of piecrust. Wet the edges of the crust with your finger, fold the crust over, and press it to seal. Place the hand pies on the prepared baking sheet and brush with the canola oil. Sprinkle with the coarse sugar.

3. Bake for 25 to 30 minutes, until golden brown. Let cool slightly before eating.

BUDGET TRICK: This recipe is perfect for using those last berries left over in their containers. You could even dice and freeze them until needed.

PER SERVING: Calories: 253; Total fat: 13g; Sodium: 406mg; Carbohydrates: 35g; Fiber: 2g; Sugars: 9g; Protein: <1g.

Carrot Snack Cake with Cream Cheese Frosting

SERVES 9 | PREP TIME: 15 MINUTES | COOK TIME: 25 MINUTES

Homemade cake is such a wonderful treat—but cake decorating can be a little daunting. That's why I love this snack cake. You get all the flavor of a lovingly baked homemade carrot cake with homemade cream cheese frosting but without the stress, time investment, or challenge of a full-size cake.

FOR THE CAKE

1 cup all-purpose flour

½ cup packed light brown sugar

2 tablespoons baking powder

1 teaspoon ground cinnamon

½ teaspoon ground nutmeg

½ teaspoon salt

1 large egg

½ cup 2 percent milk

¼ cup canola oil

1 cup finely grated carrot

TO MAKE THE CAKE

1. Preheat the oven to 375°F.

2. In a large bowl, sift together the flour, brown sugar, baking powder, cinnamon, nutmeg, and salt. Add the egg, milk, and canola oil and whisk thoroughly to combine. Stir in the carrot. Pour the batter into an 8-by-8-inch glass baking dish.

3. Bake for 20 to 22 minutes, or until a toothpick inserted into the center of the cake comes out clean. Let cool completely.

TO MAKE THE CREAM CHEESE FROSTING

4. In the bowl of a stand mixer or in a large bowl and using a handheld electric mixer, combine the butter, cream cheese, and confectioners' sugar. Mix on the lowest speed until just incorporated. Increase the speed to medium-high and beat until smooth and fluffy, about 3 minutes.

5. Add the vanilla and mix again to blend. Spread the frosting over the cake. Cut into 9 squares to serve.

FOR THE CREAM CHEESE FROSTING

8 tablespoons (1 stick)
  unsalted butter, at
  room temperature

4 ounces cream
  cheese, at room
  temperature

⅔ cup confectioners'
  sugar

1 teaspoon
  vanilla extract

BUDGET TRICK: Never buy grated carrots. Not only is it less expensive to grate your own, you can control how finely they are grated—and, in this cake, the finer, the better.

PER SERVING: Calories: 336; Total fat: 22g; Sodium: 522mg; Carbohydrates: 39g; Fiber: 1g; Sugars: 22g; Protein: 4g.

Brown Sugar Cinnamon Peach Crumble

SERVES 4 | PREP TIME: 15 MINUTES | COOK TIME: 50 MINUTES

After a spicy meal, like the Chipotle, Sweet Potato, and Black Bean Enchilada Casserole (page 60), I love to serve a sweet, fruity dessert like this one. Sweet peaches are topped with a buttery, sweet topping in this easy dessert recipe. It's decadent served with a scoop of vanilla ice cream—especially while the crumble is still hot.

3 cups frozen sliced peaches

2 tablespoons granulated sugar

2 teaspoons ground cinnamon, divided

Pinch salt

½ cup old-fashioned oats

¼ cup all-purpose flour

¼ cup packed light brown sugar

4 tablespoons cold unsalted butter, cut into pieces

1. Preheat the oven to 350°F.

2. In a pie plate, combine the peaches, granulated sugar, 1 teaspoon of cinnamon, and salt.

3. In a medium bowl, combine the oats, flour, remaining 1 teaspoon of cinnamon, and brown sugar. Add the butter pieces. Using a pastry cutter or two knives, cut the butter into the flour mixture until coarse crumbs form. Sprinkle the crumbs over the peaches.

4. Bake for 45 to 50 minutes, or until bubbly at the edges and golden brown on top.

BUDGET TRICK: **Frozen peaches are available in the freezer section of many grocery stores, but freezing your own is a great budget-friendly option. For best results, peel and slice the peaches and then freeze them on a baking sheet lined with wax paper before transferring to airtight freezer-safe bags or containers.**

PER SERVING: Calories: 281; Total fat: 12g; Sodium: 27mg; Carbohydrates: 48g; Fiber: 3g; Sugars: 27g; Protein: 3g.

Monster Peanut Butter–Chocolate Cookie Bars

SERVES 15 | PREP TIME: 20 MINUTES | COOK TIME: 30 MINUTES

Calling all peanut butter lovers! These monster cookie bars are packed with peanut butter—not only is the cookie dough part peanut butter, but the bars are dotted with chocolate peanut butter pieces, too. Plus, there's more chocolate and oats to make them really hearty and tasty. These are a sweet treat perfect for serving a crowd.

8 tablespoons (1 stick) unsalted butter, at room temperature

1 cup packed light brown sugar

½ cup peanut butter

2 large eggs

1½ cups all-purpose flour

1 cup old-fashioned oats

1 teaspoon baking powder

½ teaspoon salt

½ cup candy-coated chocolate pieces

½ cup candy-coated peanut butter chocolate pieces

1. Preheat the oven to 350°F.

2. In the bowl of a stand mixer or in a large bowl and using a handheld electric mixer, combine the butter, brown sugar, and peanut butter. Beat until thoroughly combined, about 2 minutes. One at a time, add the eggs, beating after each addition.

3. Add the flour, oats, baking powder, and salt. Beat on the lowest speed to incorporate, and then increase the speed to mix well.

4. Stir in the candy-coated chocolate and chocolate peanut butter pieces. Spread the batter into a 9-by-13-inch glass baking dish.

5. Bake for 25 to 30 minutes, until the top of the bars looks evenly done (it shouldn't look moist in the center) and it is an even, light golden brown color.

6. Let cool for 20 minutes before cutting into squares and serving.

PER SERVING: Calories: 290; Total fat: 15g; Sodium: 181mg; Carbohydrates: 41g; Fiber: 2g; Sugars: 22g; Protein: 6g.

Stuffed Baked Apples

SERVES 4 | PREP TIME: 10 MINUTES | COOK TIME: 30 MINUTES

Baking apples renders them warm, tender, and pleasing. Adding a sweet crumble filling transforms the simple apples into an elegant dish perfect for a celebration. Use a sharp knife to core the apples, or if you have one, an apple corer makes quick work of the task.

Nonstick cooking spray

4 Granny Smith apples, cored

½ cup old-fashioned oats

¼ cup packed, light brown sugar

2 tablespoons all-purpose flour

1 teaspoon ground cinnamon

Pinch salt

4 tablespoons unsalted butter, melted

1. Preheat the oven to 400°F. Coat an 8-by-8-inch glass baking dish with nonstick cooking spray.

2. Arrange the apples in the prepared baking dish.

3. In a medium bowl, stir together the oats, brown sugar, flour, cinnamon, and salt. Drizzle in the melted butter and mix vigorously to combine. You want to coat all the ingredients with the butter. Using a small spoon, evenly divide the filling among the apples, pressing it into the core with a clean finger. It's okay to have some piled on top of the apples as well.

4. Bake for 25 to 30 minutes, until the apples are softened and the filling is golden brown on top.

BUDGET TRICK: Always check the per unit price of apples before buying. Sometimes buying loose apples is less expensive. Sometimes buying a bag of apples is less.

PER SERVING: Calories: 300; Total fat: 13g; Sodium: 29mg; Carbohydrates: 53g; Fiber: 6g; Sugars: 33g; Protein: 2g.

5 INGREDIENTS | DAIRY-FREE | GLUTEN-FREE | NO-COOK | NUT-FREE | VEGAN

Watermelon-Kiwi Ice

SERVES 4 | PREP TIME: 10 MINUTES, PLUS 3 TO 4 HOURS FREEZING

With just two ingredients, you can create a chilled treat made entirely of fruit for a wonderful, easy dessert. Of course, when it comes to a dessert like this, patience is the secret ingredient.

4 cups cubed watermelon

2 kiwi, peeled and cut into pieces

1. In a blender, combine the watermelon and kiwi. Blend until smooth. Pour the mixture into a freezer-safe bowl with a lid. Cover and freeze for 3 to 4 hours, scraping the mixture about once every hour with a fork until frozen.

2. Scrape again with a fork to make it scoopable for serving.

BUDGET TRICK: When it comes to watermelon, skip the convenient packages of pre-cut melon. They come with a hefty premium. Instead, reach for the watermelon quarters or whole melons, which will be cheaper and come with more fruit to enjoy in other ways.

PER SERVING: Calories: 69; Total fat: <1g; Sodium: 4mg; Carbohydrates: 17g; Fiber: 2g; Sugars: 13g; Protein: 1g.

Easy Chocolate-Coconut Pudding

SERVES 4 | PREP TIME: 5 MINUTES | COOK TIME: 15 MINUTES | CHILL TIME: 1 HOUR

Creamy and chocolaty, this pudding is a favorite of my kids. Spoon it into bowls or fill mini pie shells and top with dessert topping for an extra-special treat.

1 (14-ounce) can coconut milk

⅓ cup sugar

¼ cup cocoa powder

2 tablespoons cornstarch

In a medium saucepan over medium heat, stir together the coconut milk, sugar, cocoa powder, and cornstarch. Bring the mixture to a boil, reduce the heat to medium-low, and cook, stirring, for 2 to 3 minutes, or until thickened. Transfer to a bowl, cover, and chill for 1 hour before serving.

BUDGET TRICK: **Cocoa powder and cornstarch are two pantry items with long shelf lives. Don't be afraid to buy a more cost-effective larger package of either, even if you don't use them that often.**

PER SERVING: Calories: 266; Total fat: 18g; Sodium: 26mg; Carbohydrates: 25g; Fiber: 2g; Sugars: 18g; Protein: 2g.

|||||||||||||||||||||||||||||||||||||||||||||||||||||||||||||||||||||||||||||||||||||||||||||||||||||||||||||||||||||

CHAPTER TEN

Condiments, Sauces, and Dressings

|||||||||||||||||||||||||||||||||||||||||||||||||||||||||||||||||||||||||||||||||||||||||||||||||||||||||||||||||||||

Slow Cooker Chicken Stock

MAKES ABOUT 8 CUPS | PREP TIME: 5 MINUTES | COOK TIME: 10 HOURS

Roast chicken is a delightful dish to dig into. Leftovers are great for lunches—but that's not all. Don't discard the bones! Instead, use them and add an onion to create a flavorful chicken stock perfect for making soups, stews, gravies, and dishes like Sweet and Sour Cabbage Kielbasa Soup (page 34). This chicken stock is also ideal for freezing and using later.

1 chicken carcass (such as from leftover Orange-Thyme Roast Chicken [page 78])

1 onion, quartered

8 to 10 cups water

1. Place the chicken carcass in a slow cooker and arrange the onion quarters around the chicken. Add the water until the level comes about 1 inch from the rim of the pot.

2. Cover the cooker and cook on high heat for 6 hours, or for a richer broth, cook for 8 to 10 hours, until the chicken breaks down (touch it— it should fall apart).

3. Using a fine-mesh strainer, strain the solids and transfer the stock to freezer containers (empty pasta sauce jars work well), leaving at least 1 inch at the top for expansion. Keep frozen for 6 to 9 months.

BUDGET TRICK: **Don't want to use a whole onion for this? Freeze the ends of your onions in a freezer-safe bag and toss in an amount equivalent to one onion instead.**

COOKING TIP: The benefit of making this in a slow cooker is the long cook time without any babysitting needed, which results in a rich stock. However, it can also be made on the stovetop. In a large stockpot over medium-high heat, combine the chicken carcass, onion quarters, and water. Bring to a boil and cover the pot. Reduce the heat to medium and cook, still boiling, for 2 to 3 hours, stirring occasionally, until the chicken carcass breaks down. If the water level gets low, add more water.

PER SERVING (1 CUP): Calories: 55; Total fat: 2g; Sodium: 49mg; Carbohydrates: 1g; Fiber: 0g; Sugars: 0g; Protein: 6g.

Veggie Scraps Vegetable Stock

MAKES ABOUT 8 CUPS | PREP TIME: 5 MINUTES | COOK TIME: 3 HOURS

When you purchase vegetable stock at the grocery store, it costs $2 to $4 per 4 cups. But when you make it at home, it's practically free (except for the time to cook it). Why wouldn't you make your own?

8 cups vegetable scraps

10 cups water

1. In a large stockpot over high heat, combine the vegetable scraps and water. Bring to a boil and cover the pot. Reduce the heat to medium and cook, still boiling, for 2 to 3 hours, stirring occasionally, until the vegetables are broken down. If the water level gets low, add more water.

2. Using a fine-mesh strainer, strain the solids and transfer the stock to freezer containers, leaving at least 1 inch at the top for expansion. Keep frozen for 6 to 9 months.

BUDGET TRICK: **Make a habit of saving your vegetable peels and ends. Keep a reusable bag in the freezer and tuck them all in there. When it's full, make stock; then return the bag to the freezer to refill.**

PER SERVING (1 CUP): Calories: 14; Total fat: 0g; Sodium: 14mg; Carbohydrates: 3g; Fiber: 1g; Sugars: 0g; Protein: 1g.

Ramen Broth

SERVES 1 | PREP TIME: 5 MINUTES | COOK TIME: 5 MINUTES

On the most budget-stretched days, ramen noodles are a godsend. But the seasoning packets that come with them leave a lot to be desired. Skip the packet and make this flavorful broth with pantry ingredients. Then stir in the cooked noodles, any vegetable odds and ends you have, and whatever else you'd like.

1 cup Veggie Scraps Vegetable Stock (page 138) or store-bought vegetable broth

1 tablespoon hoisin sauce

1 teaspoon soy sauce

½ teaspoon garlic powder

Few drops hot sauce

In a small saucepan over medium heat, whisk the vegetable stock, hoisin sauce, soy sauce, and garlic powder to combine. Sprinkle in the hot sauce as you like. Bring to a boil. Pour into a bowl and use as desired.

BUDGET TRICK: **Any stock or broth will work in this recipe—use what you have on hand.**

PER SERVING: Calories: 57; Total fat: 1g; Sodium: 572mg; Carbohydrates: 12g; Fiber: 2g; Sugars: 4g; Protein: 2g.

Creamy Tahini Vinaigrette

SERVES 4 | PREP TIME: 10 MINUTES

Tahini is a paste made from sesame seeds that has a strong sesame taste. When combined with seasoned rice vinegar, orange juice, and ginger, the flavor is mellowed, and it lends a creaminess to the vinaigrette without the use of dairy. This fragrant dressing is particularly good on roasted vegetables.

⅓ **cup seasoned rice vinegar**

¼ **cup olive oil**

2 **tablespoons tahini or peanut butter**

2 **tablespoons freshly squeezed orange juice**

1 **teaspoon ground ginger**

In a small bowl, whisk the vinegar, olive oil, tahini, orange juice, and ginger to combine thoroughly. Refrigerate any leftovers in an airtight container and use within 5 days.

BUDGET TRICK: Save small glass containers, wash them, and remove the labels. They are perfect for storing dressings like this.

PER SERVING: Calories: 195; Total fat: 18g; Sodium: 326mg; Carbohydrates: 9g; Fiber: 1g; Sugars: 7g; Protein: 1g.

Zesty Orange-Thyme Vinaigrette

SERVES 4 | PREP TIME: 10 MINUTES

Bright and fragrant, this light vinaigrette is wonderful for drizzling on salads. It can also be used to dress steamed vegetables.

¼ cup olive oil

Juice of 1 orange

2 tablespoons white wine vinegar

1 teaspoon dried thyme

½ teaspoon salt

¼ teaspoon freshly ground black pepper

2 or 3 drops hot sauce

In a small bowl, vigorously whisk the olive oil, orange juice, vinegar, thyme, salt, pepper, and hot sauce to combine. Refrigerate any leftovers in an airtight container and use within 4 or 5 days.

BUDGET TRICK: Did you make Orange-Thyme Roast Chicken (page 78) this week? Use the zested orange from that recipe to make this vinaigrette.

PER SERVING: Calories: 126; Total fat: 14g; Sodium: 291mg; Carbohydrates: 1g; Fiber: <1g; Sugars: 1g; Protein: <1g.

Sun-Dried Tomato-Garlic Vinaigrette $

SERVES 4 | PREP TIME: 10 MINUTES

With a rich, tangy tomato taste, this thick vinaigrette adds so much flavor to anything it dresses. Try it on a simple salad of lettuce, tomato, and mozzarella.

⅓ cup white
  wine vinegar

¼ cup olive oil

¼ cup sun-dried
  tomatoes, dry-
  or oil-packed

1 garlic clove, peeled

½ teaspoon dried basil

½ teaspoon salt

In a blender, combine the vinegar, olive oil, sun-dried tomatoes, garlic, basil, and salt. Blend until smooth. Refrigerate any leftovers in an airtight container and use within 4 or 5 days.

BUDGET TRICK: Although dry-packed sundried tomatoes can be found inexpensively at some grocery stores, sometimes you only need a few, not a whole package. Check your grocer's olive bar for oil-packed sun-dried tomatoes and buy just what you need.

PER SERVING: Calories: 134; Total fat: 14g; Sodium: 362mg; Carbohydrates: 2g; Fiber: 1g; Sugars: 1g; Protein: 1g.

5 INGREDIENTS | 30 MINUTES | GLUTEN-FREE | NO-COOK | VEGETARIAN

Basil-Walnut Pesto

MAKES ABOUT 1 CUP | PREP TIME: 10 MINUTES

On pasta, potatoes, seafood, poultry, and more, vibrant pesto lends a bright, summery flavor. I love substituting walnuts for the traditional pine nuts, as they tend to be a bit less expensive but offer a similar flavor.

2 cups packed, fresh basil leaves, rinsed and patted dry

1 garlic clove, peeled

¼ cup walnuts

¼ cup grated Romano cheese

½ cup olive oil

Salt

1. In a blender, combine the basil, garlic, walnuts, and Romano cheese. Process until chopped.

2. With the blender running, slowly add the olive oil in a thin stream, blending until incorporated. Taste and season with salt as needed.

BUDGET TRICK: **Did you know pesto freezes well? Make a big batch of pesto and freeze it in smaller portions. Better yet, grow your own basil in a pot—it's easy, and the cost of the recipe will reduce significantly.**

PER SERVING (2 TABLESPOONS):
Calories: 163; Total fat: 18g; Sodium: 64mg;
Carbohydrates: 1g; Fiber: 1g; Sugars: <1g; Protein: 2g.

Chipotle Brown Sugar Barbecue Sauce

MAKES ABOUT 2 CUPS | PREP TIME: 10 MINUTES | COOK TIME: 20 MINUTES

Sure, it's easy and inexpensive to buy barbecue sauce. But if you have leftover chipotle peppers from recipes in this book, like Spicy Chipotle Butternut Squash Soup (page 30), put them to good use in this rich homemade barbecue sauce with a kick. You control the ingredients—and it's easy to make and fun to say you did it yourself.

1 (6-ounce) can tomato paste

¼ cup molasses

¼ cup water

¼ cup packed light brown sugar

2 tablespoons apple cider vinegar

1 canned chipotle pepper in adobo sauce

1 teaspoon salt

½ teaspoon dry mustard

½ teaspoon garlic powder

½ teaspoon onion powder

1. In a medium saucepan over medium heat, whisk the tomato paste, molasses, water, brown sugar, vinegar, chipotle, salt, dry mustard, garlic powder, and onion powder. Cook, whisking, until the mixture comes to a boil.

2. Reduce the heat to medium-low and cook, whisking, for 10 to 15 minutes more, until thickened. Refrigerate any leftovers in an airtight container for up to 2 months.

BUDGET TRICK: Have leftover chipotle peppers after making this? They freeze well. Put what's left, including the sauce, into a freezer-safe container and freeze until you need them again.

PER SERVING (2 TABLESPOONS): Calories: 38; Total fat: <1g; Sodium: 241mg; Carbohydrates: 11g; Fiber: 1g; Sugars: 9g; Protein: 1g.

5 INGREDIENTS | 30 MINUTES | DAIRY-FREE | GLUTEN-FREE | NUT-FREE | ONE POT | VEGAN

Easy Marinara Sauce

MAKES ABOUT 2 CUPS | PREP TIME: 5 MINUTES | COOK TIME: 15 MINUTES

It's so easy to make your own marinara sauce with a few pantry ingredients. You might even have everything already. And feel free to make this your own, such as by adding fresh herbs, a splash of red wine, or diced tomato.

1 (6-ounce) can tomato paste

1½ cups water

1 teaspoon dried basil

1 teaspoon garlic powder

1 teaspoon onion powder

1 bay leaf

Salt

Freshly ground black pepper

1. In a medium saucepan over medium heat, stir together the tomato paste, water, basil, garlic powder, onion powder, and bay leaf. Season with salt and pepper. Bring to a boil, stirring occasionally.

2. Reduce the heat to medium-low, cover the pan, and cook for 10 minutes. Remove from heat. Refrigerate any leftovers in an airtight container for up to 1 week.

BUDGET TRICK: **No garlic powder? Substitute 1 garlic clove, minced, mixing it in as you would the garlic powder.**

PER SERVING (½ CUP): Calories: 40; Total fat: <1g; Sodium: 336mg; Carbohydrates: 9g; Fiber: 2g; Sugars: 5g; Protein: 2g.

Measurement Conversions

	US STANDARD	US STANDARD (OUNCES)	METRIC (APPROXIMATE)
VOLUME EQUIVALENTS (LIQUID)	2 tablespoons	1 fl. oz.	30 mL
	¼ cup	2 fl. oz.	60 mL
	½ cup	4 fl. oz.	120 mL
	1 cup	8 fl. oz.	240 mL
	1½ cups	12 fl. oz.	355 mL
	2 cups or 1 pint	16 fl. oz.	475 mL
	4 cups or 1 quart	32 fl. oz.	1 L
	1 gallon	128 fl. oz.	4 L
VOLUME EQUIVALENTS (DRY)	⅛ teaspoon	———	0.5 mL
	¼ teaspoon	———	1 mL
	½ teaspoon	———	2 mL
	¾ teaspoon	———	4 mL
	1 teaspoon	———	5 mL
	1 tablespoon	———	15 mL
	¼ cup	———	59 mL
	⅓ cup	———	79 mL
	½ cup	———	118 mL
	⅔ cup	———	156 mL
	¾ cup	———	177 mL
	1 cup	———	235 mL
	2 cups or 1 pint	———	475 mL
	3 cups	———	700 mL
	4 cups or 1 quart	———	1 L
	½ gallon	———	2 L
	1 gallon	———	4 L
WEIGHT EQUIVALENTS	½ ounce	———	15 g
	1 ounce	———	30 g
	2 ounces	———	60 g
	4 ounces	———	115 g
	8 ounces	———	225 g
	12 ounces	———	340 g
	16 ounces or 1 pound	———	455 g

	FAHRENHEIT (F)	CELSIUS (C) (APPROXIMATE)
OVEN TEMPERATURES	250°F	120°C
	300°F	150°C
	325°F	180°C
	375°F	190°C
	400°F	200°C
	425°F	220°C
	450°F	230°C

Index

Acknowledgments

Writing a cookbook isn't a solitary act. It requires the understanding and support of a lot of people—but especially those who eat the things I cook. Thank you to my children, Will and Paige, for the support, gentle nudging, and encouragement to keep going throughout the process. Thank you to Gibran Graham as well for enthusiastically eating so many different dishes and lending his critical editor eyes when I needed a second read.

I am also grateful to my siblings, Zach and Haley, for letting me bounce ideas off them and filling me in on what it's like to be a college and graduate student on a budget these days. It helped tremendously. Thank you also to my parents, Sue and Rick, for everything.

Every book I write has a soundtrack. Usually it's pretty specific, but this time it was the nominees for the 2020 Grammy Awards. A special debt of gratitude goes to Lewis Capaldi, whose song "Someone You Loved" broke me free of more than one bout of writer's block.

Over the course of my career, I've been lucky enough to be handed a few proposals that so perfectly matched both my experience and my frame of mind. This was one of them. Thank you to the Callisto team for selecting me for this project and helping shepherd it to completion.

About the Author

SARAH WALKER CARON is an award-winning food columnist and writer and the voice behind the popular food blog *Sarah's Cucina Bella* (SarahsCucinaBella .com). She began writing about food in 2005 after her son Will was born. Since then, her work and writing have appeared in countless publications, including *Fine Cooking*, *Bella Magazine*, *Yum for Kids*, BettyCrocker .com, and SheKnows.com. She is the author of *The Super Easy 5-Ingredient Cookbook*, *One-Pot Pasta*, *The Easy Appetizer Cookbook, Classic Diners of Maine,* and co-author of *Grains as Mains*: *Modern Recipes Using Ancient Grains*. She also writes cooking columns for *Bangor Metro* magazine and *The Bangor Daily News*. Named the 2015 Maine local columnist of the year by the Maine Press Association, Sarah is a graduate of Barnard College and lives in Maine with her two kids and black cat named Bippity.

CPSIA information can be obtained
at www.ICGtesting.com
Printed in the USA
JSHW031932300620
6375JS00007B/3